# Every Man's Survival Guide
# to Ballroom Dancing

# Every Man's Survival Guide to Ballroom Dancing

**Ace Your Wedding Dance and Keep Cool on a Cruise, at a Formal, and in Dance Classes**

## James Joseph

**IMPORTANT NOTE TO THE READER:** Dancing, like any other form of exercise, can cause serious injury. For that reason, the reader is encouraged to consult a physician before undertaking a dancing or dance instruction program. Readers should always take care to avoid injuring themselves and others. Please be a gentle, responsible dancer and always take care of your partner. The author and publisher disclaim any responsibility or liability for injury or loss that may result, whether directly or indirectly, from using the contents of this book.

The author and publisher gratefully acknowledge the permission granted by Skippy Blair and the Golden State Dance Teachers Association (GSDTA) to access, quote and make reference to materials created by Skippy Blair. For more information, please contact the GSDTA at (562) 869-8949 or swingworld.com.

Cover and interior design by Barbara Balch.
Cover photo by Gregory Costanzo/Getty Images.
Back cover photo by Young-Sun Teh/BigStockPhoto.com.

ISBN 978-0-930251-44-4
Library of Congress Control Number: 2009908151

BlueChip Publishers
Jackson Hole, Wyoming
BlueChipPublishers.com
Available for purchase in bulk and in custom editions.

Go to ihatetodance.com for video clips, blog, updates, and corrections to the book.

Version 1.0

I am grateful and deeply indebted to dance educator Skippy Blair for her guidance and the unlimited access that she granted me to material she developed for the Golden State Dance Teachers Association (GSDTA), including her classic work, *Dance Terminology Notebook*, which is available on her website (swingworld.com). I want to give her ample credit for her contribution to the field of dance instruction, and I have tried to point out to the reader whenever I use one of the terms she coined or refer to a concept that she taught to generations of dancers and dance instructors.

Skippy did not read the final manuscript of the book, and she did not approve or disapprove of what I have written. This book is not about Skippy Blair's system of dance, and it reflects my own experience and my own interpretation only. However, Skippy was generous and encouraging throughout the process of researching and writing this book, and I want to honor her as a pioneering figure in dance and thank her for the permission she has graciously extended to me to make use of the information and materials she shared with me.

I was not a typical student for Skippy. I wasn't a teacher, I wasn't a competitor and I wasn't into West Coast swing, her primary dance (Skippy is credited with first using the name, West Coast swing, in an advertisement in the early 1960s). I was just someone who needed to make sense of all the nonsensical information I had been fed over the years. I connected with her immediately, because she had a logical method for teaching music and rhythm, the same techniques she uses to train world-class competitors. Without Skippy Blair I would still be rhythmically challenged, oblivious to the beat of the music. I now enjoy music more because of her. Without Skippy I'd still be the guy at the wedding, lurking in the corner, hiding from the dance floor. Skippy pulled me out of that dark shadow. Because of Skippy Blair, I now know how to satisfy a woman on the dance floor.

Props to Kate Ford who kept me going over the years. A shout-out to John from Seattle (see Chapter 2), who first made me realize that I was missing something in my training (it's not a coincidence that his training traces back to Skippy Blair). Thanks to my editors, Dick Margulis and Robin Miura, my book designer, Barbara Balch, and my book maven, Ina Stern.

# Contents

TO FELICE

# 10 Tips to Fred Astairedom

Can't act. Can't sing. Slightly bald.
Can dance a little.

*— Goldwyn (predecessor to MGM) talent scout's*
*assessment of Fred Astaire, famous film actor, dancer*
*and cofounder of Fred Astaire Dance Studios*

This book is for non-dancers, newbies and beginners. If you can't dance or fear dance or hate to dance, I can help. I'm a survivor.

As someone who used to freak out at the thought of dancing, and finished countless dance classes more confused than when he started, I needed this book *before* stepping onto the floor, as well as to guide me through the first year. While women will find plenty in here to take away, this book is written for men, especially untalented and rhythmically challenged men. We have been ignored and we need help.

The aim of *Every Man's Survival Guide to Ballroom Dancing* is not so much to learn salsa or waltz or jitterbug—you should take lessons for specific dances you want to learn well. Part guerrilla manual and part cotillion handbook, the purpose here is simpler and more practical: to learn the basic principles common to all music and dance, enabling you to walk onto any dance floor, from a nightclub to a wedding to a cruise to a New Year's Eve ball, and to perform an admirable dance, with any partner, to any music, with confidence and grace.

I speak from experience: Many times I have frozen rigor-mortis-stiff at the edge of a dance floor. I stood in fear not only that I would request a dance and be rejected, but that my request would

### How to Fake a Dance

If you're in a rush, what you need is a quick course in how to fake ballroom dancing. Having wished for that course a million times myself, I give suggestions in Chapter 15, "16 Tips for Surviving a Dance."

There's no need to panic, really. Most men—and most women—can't dance, so the challenge of satisfying your partner on an unsophisticated dance floor, like a wedding reception, may not be as hard as you think. I explore this further in "The Last Word: Reality Check" at the end of the book.

be accepted, I would be revealed as a dance-fraud and a buffoon, and they would tattoo the big L for loser on my forehead.

Occasionally, I still have trepidations and self-doubt, but now I know the protocol and can keep my cool—and dance comfortably with anyone, anywhere, to any music, under the most adverse conditions imaginable. So can you.

## USING THIS BOOK

While this book is aimed at beginners, beginners are a diverse bunch. Sometimes I talk to the new dancer and sometimes I talk to the guy who's been at it for a while but is frustrated. Sometimes I talk to the beginner who gets it, kind of, but he's plateaued and needs a push to get him to the intermediate level. Sometimes I talk to the groom who just wants to get through his wedding, and sometimes I talk to the alpha-male-in-training who's hopelessly challenged but committed to becoming the Don Juan of the dance floor. If you find material that doesn't relate to you or that's above your head, no sweat; just bookmark it for later with a sticky note and push forward. I've tried to identify the harder stuff with the label **ADVANCED INFO ALERT** (see "Alerts and Other Thingies"). Still, people have different learning styles and different endgames so adjust accordingly.

## Alerts and Other Thingies

### ADVANCED INFO ALERT

Identifies information that's above the first-time-dancer beginner level. When you're ready, this stuff will help you move to the next level. In addition to Advanced Info Alerts, sometimes I just tell you when a section is more difficult material.

### Lingo Alert

Many, many times I've tripped over conflicting and confusing language as I learned to dance. I've identified my bugaboos and, hopefully, saved you some grief.

### TIPS

Boy, do I like tips. There are even a few tips for the ladies.

### EXERCISES

There are 17 exercises. They're pretty easy and most don't require a partner. Repetition will set you free.

### Definitions

Important words are called out in the text. The language of dance may be daunting to some, so there's a short glossary at the back of the book. The words are arranged in roughly the order they appear in the book, not alphabetically, which keeps related words next to each other. It makes a good review, even if it's a wacky way to organize a glossary.

### Freebie Video

Dance begs for video, and I have delivered—sort of. If you check out my website, ihatetodance.com, you'll find links to some free, short, homemade videos. Spielberg I'm not.

In addition to video clips at ihatetodance.com, you can also check out my blog, ask me questions, give me corrections, get corrections, get updates and vent your frustration.

If you take classes in conjunction with this book, note that instructors have different methods of teaching, so you may encounter diverse opinions on what's right and wrong. As with most things in life, learn all that you can from whomever you can, think about it, practice, discover what works best and develop your own style. In that light, look at this book more as a starting point or a waypoint, not as an end point, to your journey.

For the record, *Every Man's Survival Guide to Ballroom Dancing* is written for *social dancing*—dancing for fun—and not for winning competitions. The competitive world of dance plays by a lot of rules that are not relevant to the social dancer. For comparison, it would be an exasperating existence if we had to conform to racewalking regulations just to walk around the block.

## 10 TIPS

You decide you want to make mincemeat out of *Dirty Dancing* stars Patrick Swayze and Jennifer Grey. What next?

Regrettably, you can't buy the recognition of high-performance dancing like you can buy a Harley. It'll be a process and, as in the pursuit of any sport or art, it's best to focus on the activity and not on the destination. Dance at any level has some rewards.

I stumbled along as a beginner, in the dark, for many years. I had ample time to ponder the problems. What follows are the elements of learning to dance that helped the most, that got me into the limelight. Alrighty then, it's show time . . .

**1.** *Understand the music.* I heard this directive—understand the music—many times from great dancers. It initially struck me as lame advice since listening to music didn't seem too productive—after all, I had listened my whole life and, heck, it hadn't done beans. Now I can't stress this one enough for the newbie: listen actively to lots of music. In particular, learn how to count the beats of music to identify the musical structure. The experts say dance is a three-way partnership between you, your partner and the music. Know the music well.

*Bonus Tip:* Find music you love. Big band, blues, Latin, salsa, waltz, soul, rock 'n roll, cha-cha, hip-hop, country and western, top 40. Find specific songs that you love. See what social dance fits this music and learn it first. Always try to dance to music you love; it makes dancing so much easier.

**2.** *Take lessons.* Can you learn to land the space shuttle without lessons? Same with dance (well, almost). You need quality instruction, preferably both classes and, if you're serious about learning to dance, occasional private lessons. Not only will you need a teacher to demonstrate those elements of music and dance that defy words, you'll need someone to tell you when you're doing something right or wrong—no book, video or DVD alone can do that. There are different ways to teach, so it's best to sample what's out there and choose a teacher who matches your style and needs.

*Bonus Tip:* After a six-week beginners' class most people progress to the intermediate series. Then, after the six-week intermediate class, they think they're intermediate dancers. Not! Just knowing some intermediate step patterns and 12 weeks of training does not make you an intermediate dancer. Consider taking the beginners' class several times before moving on to the intermediate series (or take it again in conjunction with intermediate classes).

**3.** *Focus on rhythm patterns, not direction of movement.* A *step pattern*—those fancy-looking moves that define a dance— is the bigger motion a couple makes on the floor. It combines a *direction*, which is where to move, with a *rhythm pattern*, which is when to make weight changes. A rhythm pattern, which can be practiced by stepping in place (also known as *marking* a rhythm), has to do with whether you step or don't step on a beat of music and whether you get fancy and step between beats of music, not the geography created when you move around the floor. For the beginner, I believe understanding when to step (rhythm patterns) is far more important than where to step (direction). Rhythm patterns—not to be confused with the rhythmic beat of the music—are the focus of this book.

**4.** *Focus on technique, not learning more step patterns.* If a step pattern is the fancy move you do on the floor, technique is how you do it. Technique is the subtle movements of the body that improve the look of the step pattern. Most newbies are focused just on what foot to move and where to move it. But remember to pay attention when your teacher tells you how to move your body, how to improve the lead and how to make it look better. Please, look beyond the superficial accumulation of patterns; see that good technique looks better than an encyclopedic memory and regurgitation of sloppy patterns. Understand that a well-executed, simple step pleases the eye—and your partner—more than a poorly executed, eye-catching pattern. Partners will line up for the guy with a handful of perfect patterns as quickly as they will avoid the schlub with dozens of reckless steps.

**5.** *Get out and dance.* This book should help a great deal, but don't expect miracles: you can't learn to dance just from reading a book. You must get out and dance, even occasionally, because any time on the floor will make you better. With great music and enjoyable partners, the work is easy.

*Bonus Tip:* "Shadow dancing" at home, alone, counts for time on the floor too. See page 123.

**6.** *Dance with a variety of partners.* Having a regular partner is groovy and will accelerate your progress. But as a beginner, dancing with only one person over time might result in bad habits. It's important to have a variety of partners, as adjusting to a new partner is a basic dance skill. If you're shy, finding any partner is a challenge. Taking classes is a good route as it removes the stress of finding a partner.

**7.** *Dance up.* By *dancing up* I mean asking better dancers than you to dance. As a beginner, the vast majority of your partners will be at your level; dancing up is something to do occasionally (careful: if you do it a lot and ignore partners at your level, people may think you have an attitude). If you're a beginner and only dance with partners of equal ability (read: little ability), often stuff won't work; it's easy to assume you're at fault, a bad dancer. When you dance up, miraculously, things begin to work, and you're able to move to the next level. You should dance up, occasionally, if you want to progress at a reasonable rate. Later, when you can dance, it's payback time: Go out of your way to dance with dancers not as good as you.

*Bonus Tip:* Here's an easy way to dance up: after a class, tell the teacher you're not sure if you got a step pattern; ask the teacher to demonstrate it with you so you can feel it done correctly.

**8.** *Recover seamlessly from missteps.* As a beginner, you'll make plenty of missteps and minor slips. Handling them is tough—it's not always clear why something went wrong—and the poor handling of slipups is a common cause of bad feelings.

---

### *The Original Speed Dating*

At its core partner dancing is a mating ritual, and many people pursue dance just to get dates. In recent years, swing and salsa classes have overflowed with singles looking for love. The ability to dance has always been a good way to attract attention from the opposite sex, and dancing is a good way to quickly meet a lot of ladies. After all, the average song is just three minutes long; you can log a couple dozen dances in an evening.

Socially awkward? Don't have the gift of gab? No problem. Once again, dance to the rescue. Dance is mostly nonverbal and it includes a ploy to say hello with a mandatory script: "Hi, would you like to dance?" Not that forward? A dance class that regularly rotates partners will put 6, 8 or 10 ladies in your hands in an hour, with no effort and risk-free.

## Bruce Lee, Martial Artist or Dancer?

He was both. Legendary martial artist Bruce Lee was the cha-cha champion of Hong Kong in 1958. Coincidence? Although we don't see him dance, the first fight scene in the movie *Dragon: The Bruce Lee Story* occurs at a dance, in the middle of a cha-cha. Pow!

Lighten up, dude, nobody is at fault. It's best not to blame, and if you're the culprit, do not apologize excessively. Dance right through mistakes. In fact, recovering from a stumble is a critical skill every advanced dancer can do. Such accidents can even be fun and produce interesting results—add a smile and it may look like you were improvising a new move. Don't be afraid to make a mistake.

*Bonus Tip:* Even in a practice session, when it's agreed upon to call attention to your partner's mistakes, it's still a good idea to be diplomatic, for example: "That didn't feel quite right to me. How did it feel to you?"

**9.** *Watch great dancers.* By watching great dancers you develop a sense of the possibilities, you begin to define your personal style and you create an image in your mind of where you want to go. Like salivating at the thought of food, a mental image can affect us physically: by observing and saturating your psyche with great dancing and visualizing your goals, you'll program your subconscious mind and prep your body for a better performance. It's a good activity when sitting out a dance. When I got hooked on becoming a better dancer, I stopped gazing at the women and started studying the men—to steal moves.

**10.** *Learn manners.* Yeah, I only had nine tips so this is filler, but it's good filler . . . manners, etiquette, common courtesies, the whole shebang. Be a gentle, polite dancer so you'll have lots of partners. You're allowed to be a little klutzy but not a little rude. And check your attitude: it's best to be warm and friendly with all eye contact, to treat everyone with respect. Watch that

## Heroic Men Who Dance

Growing up, one of my first impressions of dancing was from a scene in a James Bond movie. Here was one of the most heroic, debonair, masculine images of a lifetime, and there he was, dancing with a gorgeous woman. Where do I sign up? Interestingly, there's a notable list of films in the last 30 years with heroic men who dance: *Saturday Night Fever* (John Travolta), *Urban Cowboy* (John Travolta), *Dirty Dancing* (Patrick Swayze), *Malcolm X* (Denzel Washington), *Witness* (Harrison Ford), *The Mask of Zorro* (Antonio Banderas), *True Lies* (Arnold Schwarzenegger), *Mr. & Mrs. Smith* (Brad Pitt), *The Big Chill* (Kevin Kline), *A Perfect World* (Kevin Costner), *Silverado* (Kevin Costner), *Chocolat* (Johnny Depp), *The Mask* (Jim Carrey), *Scent of a Woman* (Al Pacino), *All the Pretty Horses* (Matt Damon), *Bridges of Madison County* (Clint Eastwood), *Eyes Wide Shut* (Tom Cruise), *Shall We Dance* (Richard Gere) and *The Matador* (Pierce Brosnan), to name a few.

ego does not exceed ability—this can wear thin on others, and it's hard to dance with someone when he lacks sensitivity to his partner. Think: less is more.

One more thing: make it fun, not a burden. I stressed excessively about becoming a great dancer. I had the unhealthy attitude that I didn't want to dance and embarrass myself until I was a great dancer, which was an utterly destructive catch-22: I wouldn't dance until I was good, but I couldn't get good until I danced. I now realize that there aren't a lot of Rudolph Valentinos (the tango-dancing, Latin lover, silent film star) out there—hardly any—and most women are impressed with just a gentle, adequate dancer. Once again, find fulfillment in the journey and do not fixate on the goal. To paraphrase an old Zen saying: With one eye so firmly planted on your goal, you'll only have one eye left to lead the way.

# PART 1

# Music

# Chapter 1

# The Beat of the Music

As I see it, I need to maneuver my partner around
the dance floor, taking care not to bump into anyone
or anything, dancing to the music, spontaneously
choreographing a changing and pleasing series of
moves, all the while maintaining light conversation. . . .
My, this is difficult, isn't it?

— *Mr. Data (an android),* Star Trek: The Next Generation

Find the beat. Cool step patterns that are off the beat
look bad; simple moves on the beat look cool. Don't
be that goofball on the floor who knows billions of patterns yet
dances off the beat.

Okay, in the past, more often than I want to admit, I was
that goofball. Sometimes I couldn't hear the beat, but sometimes
I swear it wasn't my fault. In my defense, and in defense of all
the beat-challenged guys who have ever stumbled through a
dance, I'd like to explain how circumstances beyond my control
conspired to dislodge me from the beat:

- There was the distraction of flirting with my partner.

- There was the distraction of trying to lead the step
  pattern I was executing.

- There was the distraction of choreographing the next
  step pattern or two in my head.

- There was the confusion of songs with an elusive
  beat (including the challenge of up-tempo songs—
  just too darn fast to stay on the beat).

- There was the anxiety of being self-conscious—the weird distraction of watching others to see if they were watching me.

My beatless years were a puzzle. For a long time I was not connected to the beat but thought I was. I now realize that I often guessed at the beat and, like a broken clock being right twice a day, was often correct. This gave me the illusion that I knew the beat, and it let my ego exceed my ability. But it took very little to dislodge my feet from the beat. Through good teachers and persistence, I eventually embraced the beat and learned to take distractions in stride. Fear not, O Humble Goofball, all beat-challenged people can get better.

The **beat** is the regular *thump thump* or *tap tap* that marks time, like the ticking of a clock. Also called the *underlying beat*, it's the pulse of the music.

**TIP** I find the beat is harder to hear in songs with a lot of drumming. For example, salsa has a lot of percussion, and it seems like fast salsa music will always be a challenge for me. Swing (big band jazz) and blues always seem to have beats that are obvious. When you practice, use music

---

### Lingo Alert: Dancers versus Musicians

Sometimes dance teachers use a musician's language to describe the underlying beat as a *quarter note*, a definition that always bugged me. I understood why it was called a quarter note but it annoyed me because it was, for the social dancer, not user-friendly. It distracted me because it made me wonder if I needed to know more, like eighth notes, half notes and whole notes (I didn't and you don't). If "quarter note" is lobbed at you, don't panic and don't overthink it; simply accept it as a synonym for the underlying beat. While it's good to know some musical terminology, dancers deal with music differently than musicians. Dancers have a simple, complementary system, just enough to connect us to the music so we can dance, not compose music and play it.

with beats that are easy to hear, because you have to hear it in the easy tunes before you can hear it in the harder stuff.

**Tempo** is the speed of the music, typically stated as slow, medium or fast. But be aware that labels, like *slow* and *medium*, are subjective—what's slow for me may be medium to you. Tempo is measured in beats per minute or BPM. *Up-tempo* refers to faster music.

I found tempo a bit of a demon. Many times I'd get good at doing a pattern in class, and that ability would mysteriously vanish at a club. I now know that up-tempo music, which is harder to dance to, was one of the major culprits. A teacher will often play slower music to teach than you would typically find at a real dance.

The beat is important because most steps (that is, weight changes, see the following Lingo Alert) for the basic patterns of every dance occur on the beat; if you're stepping slightly ahead or slightly behind the beat of the music, it's considered *off time* and it will feel uncomfortable to your partner. Of all the klutzy things you could do on the floor—short of injuring your partner—being off time will do the most harm. I don't care if you know every dance pattern in the solar system, if you're not stepping on the beat your partner will deem you . . . well, unless you're a hunky, biceptually endowed *GQ* model, someone to keep at a distance. On the bright side, even if you don't know any patterns, just step-ping on the beat as you attempt to fake it will be appreciated and make her think, *Hey, this guy's okay; he's got some rhythm.*

*Lingo Alert:* Here comes a little curveball. In this book the word *step* is synonymous with the phrase *weight change*, that is, any shift in weight from left foot to right foot or vice versa. It means the moment the weight changes and not necessarily the moment when your foot first touches the floor. So, unless I tell you otherwise, don't think of a *step* as a process, like taking a step, but think of it as an instant in time—the weight change—which, for the beginner, needs to occur precisely on a beat of music. And note that a weight transfer can be done in place, yielding a step in place, so a *step* doesn't always mean there's movement in a particular direction. One more thing: *step* is also short for *step pattern*. For example, you might say, "I learned a new step tonight." So the word *step* has to be understood in context.

You'll have to learn the beat on your own, as this is not something you will be taught in a beginners' class in foxtrot or waltz or tango at a studio. For me, classes were helpful only to the extent that after they ended I'd confess to the teachers that I wasn't sure of the beat and had them help me tap it out for 30 seconds to the practice music. I also bugged a lot of innocent bystanders, on and off the dance floor, strangers included, seeking correction and guidance—although I don't think they were really annoyed, because dancers like to show off.

For me, hearing the beat was a two-part process: first, finding the beat—just being able to stand on the sidelines and tap my foot to the beat; second, holding the beat in my body through all the distractions of dancing so that when I took a step, I stepped on the beat. While finding the beat was hard at times, it was part two, staying on the beat, that was the real problem.

I had a regular partner, a very good dancer, who would often tell me I was off the beat. Impossible! You're crazy! How could I be off the beat if I hear it? Eventually I noticed a pattern. I'd start a dance with good concentration and I'd be fine. But then my ego would kick in and I'd want to do more (read: show off). My dance ability was limited; so, choosing the next best thing, I desperately wanted to talk—to dazzle her with my wit—and dance at the same time. I would lose the beat the moment I opened my mouth. The day I could finally talk and dance at the same time was a huge milestone for me.

Both issues, hearing the beat and staying on the beat, were part of a bigger problem: What little grasp of the beat I had was only auditory or intellectual and not visceral or intuitive. Maybe I could hear the beat if I had no distractions, but I couldn't feel the beat in my body. Intuitively feeling the beat, an automatic and thoughtless process, would have allowed me both to hear the beat more readily and to feel it, even through the distractions.

The process was hard because I thought I knew the beat; I had no sense of what it was like to know it at this deeper, intuitive level. I was in denial about being rhythmically challenged. So it felt like I was going nowhere, trying to correct a nonexistent problem. People told me that I'd eventually get it, and I would think, *get what?*

My breakthrough in hearing the beat (I use hearing the beat synonymously with feeling the beat unless the context suggests otherwise) came when I was able to hear that not all beats are equal, that some beats hit the ear differently than others. Some beats are accented. That is, they stand out; and the degree and type of emphasis can vary. Typically, accented beats are just louder, with more oomph, as if instruments or vocals are hitting the note on that beat harder. But some beats sound different because they identify beginning points, like the start of a verse or a chorus or other, more subtle, thematic elements in the music. To my untrained ear I didn't always know why a beat sounded different; but, regardless of the reason, just hearing that not all beats sound the same is what I found to be important.

The neat thing about these different beats is that, if you listen carefully, they create simple, regularly occurring sequences. Yes, it was subtle; but in the background these different beats created patterns. Once I began to hear these arrangements, the beats began to show some distinction. They came alive!

There are two patterns of beats that can be heard in virtually all dance music. These patterns will help you learn the beat of the music. The first pattern, *sets of 8*, discussed in Chapter 2, "Counting Music: Finding the Sets of 8," defines the beat, which will help you find it and help confirm that you're on it. The second pattern, *downbeat* and *upbeat*, discussed in Chapter 3, "Downbeat and Upbeat," will help you stay on the beat. The next two chapters reveal the secrets to mastering the beat.

**TIP** I wish I could tell you that learning to hear the beat is simple: have someone help you tap your foot to the beat and then, on your own, just tap your foot to a variety of music for a week or two. Done. If you're good with music, perhaps it'll be that easy. For me, an average guy with scant musical ability, it took many, many months of listening, counting, tapping, marching and, most important, getting confirmation from others. Unless you're certain you're on the beat, always counting and tapping by yourself won't help; if you're off the beat you'll just reinforce the error. As you practice you must get confirmation from others. I mean that quite literally: regularly ask other dancers to test you, by observing you tap a foot, march in place or count sets of 8.

# Chapter 2

# *Counting Music: Finding the Sets of 8*

Football isn't a contact sport; it's a collision
sport. Dancing is a contact sport.

— *Vince Lombardi, legendary Green Bay Packers coach*

I was always suspicious of the counting I heard in dance classes. I like numbers, and I'm a good counter, so it was odd. Dang it all, counting confused me! Fear not, I've expended endless calories, tortured and maimed untold brain cells and burned through thousands of dollars in dance lessons to make sense of this simple subject.

I believe part of the problem revolves around what is being counted. Although they're related, *counting music* and *counting step patterns* are not the same. This chapter explores counting music; Chapter 6, "Counting Step Patterns," looks at counting step patterns. For most people, especially men or anyone who believes he or she is rhythmically challenged, I believe learning to count, both the music and step patterns, is the gateway to intermediate-level dancing and above.

For me as a beginner, counting music was hard to pin down because—well, because nobody ever told me how to do it. Not only is it rarely taught in a class, except for one situation (when a teacher counts you in to start a dance, discussed at the end of this chapter), it's rarely heard in class. And some teachers use musician lingo whenever they reference the musical count; that always threw me for a loop. Loops I didn't need.

**Counting music** is counting the underlying beats of the music. Doing so reveals the structure of the music. It pertains only to the structure of the music—not the step pattern being danced—and virtually all dance music is counted the same. The one exception is waltz, which is covered on pages 74 and 124. When I refer to "virtually all dance music," it means all dance music except the waltz.

So, forget all the highfalutin-hieroglyphic-4/4-2/4-3/4-time-signature-mumbo-jumbo-music-theory you've been bulldozed with in the past. This is the only thing you need to know: *virtually all dance music is counted in* sets of 8 *beats*. It's as simple as that. Sets of 8 exist because that's how musicians compose the music; it's how they give structure to the music. It's the same way a sentence gives structure to the written word, as you'll see in a moment. Sets of 8 are important to dancers for a number of reasons but most importantly because they identify and define the underlying beat of the music.

I remember the first time I ever heard the structure of music counted, with the help of John, a stranger at a bar. This was a big event for me. John caught my eye because the level of his dancing was high, higher than anything I'd ever observed in my local scene. I was dying to know his secret; so I approached him and asked why his dancing was so distinctive. He said he was connected to the music—through the count—and he demonstrated. We proceeded to listen to the house band, music I had listened to for years.

He counted the music in sets of 8 beats. He counted 8 beats of music—"*one* two three four *five* six seven eight"—and then started over. He emphasized each **count 1** of the music, the first beat of each set of 8, by punching the air with his hand. (And, to a lesser degree, he also emphasized each **count 5**, the fifth beat of a set of 8, with a smaller punch.) With the help of his hand motions I could hear that all the **count 1s** were, indeed, naturally emphasized in the music. (*Lingo Alert:* Sometimes the word "**count**" is omitted and a **count 1** is identified as "the **1** of the music" or just "the **1**.") Moreover, I could hear that the **1s** were *beginning points* that signaled the beginning of something new in the melody. The concept of a beginning point was subtle; but if someone identified it for me, I could hear it.

He kept track of the sets of 8 as they passed, and he identified the bigger structure of the music. He predicted and caught all the big accents and breaks in the music with his hand motions—music he claimed he was not familiar with. This went on for song after song and, with his guidance, I could hear that every song had the same basic structure of sets of 8. I thought that maybe it was a trick; perhaps he was the band's manager or something. Nope. He was just a stranger, first time in town, first time at this joint.

Not only did every song have the same structure, he claimed most popular music had this structure of sets of 8. Nahhh . . . impossible . . . surely it worked only for these songs because, well, they're all from the same band or something. I couldn't believe it would work for all songs—could it? Is it possible that I had danced for years oblivious to the common structure in virtually all dance music? Was I that detached from the music that no matter how many songs passed me by I couldn't hear the structure that now screams at me? It's remarkable that in seven years of dance lessons, nobody had done this demonstration for me before.

While it took time before I could count sets of 8 on my own to a broad spectrum of music and test this earth-shattering hypothesis, he was right: *All dance music, except waltz, shares a similar structure.* Heck, most popular music, even the gnarliest rock or rap you've ever heard, probably shares the same repeatable, predictable sets of 8 as dance music.

**Sets of 8,** which identify the underlying beat and reflect the true structure of the music, are the foundation of counting music. For beginners, counting music is done off the dance floor when you're not dancing, to help you connect to the music. Counting is simple: listen for any **count 1** to start, then count 1, 2, 3, 4, 5, 6, 7, 8. Then start over. If you want to count how many sets of 8 go by, count the second set like this: 2, 2, 3, 4, 5, 6, 7, 8; count the third like this: 3, 2, 3, 4, 5, 6, 7, 8; count the fourth set

## The Musician's Measure

I wanted to label this discussion on the musician's *measure* as an Advanced Info Alert as it may be too much information. I hate to burden the beginner with musical terms. But *measure* gets tossed around a lot among dancers, and understanding it will do a lot to help you hear the sets of 8.

A **measure,** a musical term, is a unit of time that counts virtually all dance music in groups of four beats. That's how musicians deal with dance music, and there are dancers who follow this path of four. It's a workable system for dancers . . . nahh, I take that back; just stick with sets of 8. They're easier and more accurate. Even professional dance choreographers and aerobics instructors use sets of 8, also called a "dancer's eight," to choreograph their routines.

Actually, measures are naturally paired. So a set of 8 is just a combination of two four-beat measures, but sets of 8 work better for dancers because they're more closely aligned to the natural structure. Think of the pairing of measures this way: Break a pencil in half. It's still the same pencil, and you can write with it. But it's easier to work with the whole pencil. Musicians compose music half a pencil at a time, but their goal is to create a whole pencil. It's easier for dancers to just look at the whole pencil. So, thematically, a four-beat measure, while it

like this: 4, 2, 3, 4, 5, 6, 7, 8, and so on. In this book, a set of 8 beats looks like this (note that they're in pairs, which will make sense after you read the next two chapters):

| MUSICAL COUNT | 1 | 2 | | 3 | 4 | | 5 | 6 | | 7 | 8 |
|---|---|---|---|---|---|---|---|---|---|---|---|

Whether you can hear sets of 8 or not, sets of 8 are "in" the music. Once you develop your ear, which you will over time, a set of 8 will stand out, with integrity, in much the same way a sentence stands out from within a paragraph. *Like the written word, music has themes and these themes are directly related to the musical count.* In fact, if the song has vocals, sometimes a sentence or phrase of words aligns with a set of 8.

has some integrity on its own, sounds incomplete, like half a sentence.

The order matters in the pairing of measures. There's the first half, the measure that begins the set of 8, **counts 1** to **4**; and there's the last half, the measure that ends the set of 8, **counts 5** to **8**. To hear the correct order, listen to the melody, especially the feeling that the first measure begins something and that the last measure ends it. Also, listen for the relative difference in emphasis on the **count 1** and the **count 5**. The point to note is that the **count 1** has a stronger accent than the **count 5**, which will help you distinguish between the **1** and the **5**. (Recall from earlier, I said that John, the stranger who first helped me count music, also punched out the **5s** with his hand, but to a lesser degree.) The order can be subtle—often very, very subtle—but it's there, even if you can't hear it. Like sets of 8, the natural pairing of measures is just *in* the count of the music.

Hearing accented beats, measures and sets of 8 is tricky. Depending on the music, there can be a lot going on or very little going on, which makes the process tough. But once you get it, it'll become second nature.

*Arcane Technical Info:* Some dancers count tempo in measures per minute (MPM). Multiply MPM by four to get beats per minute (BPM). Most dance music falls in a range of, say, 80 to 160 BPM, which would be 20 to 40 MPM.

For me, hearing sets of 8 is a two-part approach. First, using a more left-brain-linear-analytical approach, I try to identify the **count 1s**, the first beat of a set of 8. A **count 1** stands out because it typically has an emphasis or accent. It also stands out because it's a beginning point for a piece of the melody or other thematic element; it sounds like a natural place to start something. It's the same type of feeling you get at the start of a new sentence.

Second, using a more right-brain-holistic-intuitive approach, I listen to the overall melody of the music and try to hear the whole sentence (the whole set of 8). If I can hear, thematically, that I'm coming to the end of a sentence in the music, then I can feel when the next sentence will start. If I predict correctly, it gets confirmed by hearing the accent on the next **count 1** and the feeling that, thematically, a new sentence has started. Today, this method, feeling the music, is the primary way I connect to the sets of 8, and much of it is done subconsciously, without thinking. *Lingo Alert:* I'm going to pull a fast one with language: Don't tell any musicians but, for convenience, I tend to use the word *melody* generically to mean the themes I hear in any of the three components that combine to make a piece of music—melody, harmony or rhythm (drums).

So what's the catch? Hearing the **count 1s** and the sentence structure in the music is hard. If it were easy to hear I would have heard it on my own and you would be able to hear it on your own and we could all drop this book and go dance. Even after I realized that sets of 8 existed, it took many, many months of listening and practicing and getting confirmation from others before I could hear the structure and it became second nature. Until I could confidently count sets of 8, I was never 100 percent certain I was on the beat.

## EXERCISE 1: COUNT SETS OF 8

To get started, spend time with a teacher or friend listening to a variety of music. You can listen to your own music collection; but also surf the radio dial and music websites that let you sample music, as listening to unfamiliar songs is an important part of the process. Count the *sets of 8.* If a song stumps you, move on quickly, because you have to hear it in the easy pieces before you can hear it in the harder stuff. Do the **count 1s** stand out? Do the **1s** and **5s** seem to have the same emphasis? The beat with more emphasis, however subtle that may be, is the **1.** If you have a hard time hearing the beat, plan on sticking with this exercise for many months, working both on your own and with occasional confirmation from others.

**TIP** Sometimes vocals line up nicely with the sets of 8, sometimes not. Sometimes the accent on the **count 1** is an accented vocal, sometimes not. The beat of the music is established by the percussion instruments, like drums. In general, don't get distracted by lyrics.

**ANOTHER TIP** When practicing the beat, in addition to counting, it's always good to get some body movement. While tapping your foot is okay, the most effective way to train your body to feel the beat is marching in place, doing a weight change on every beat of music.

*Freebie Video:* Check out my website (ihatetodancec.com) for some video clips, which will help you count sets of 8.

What's so important about counting the musical structure? For me as a beginner, there were three elements. First, hearing the structure was a big step toward connecting to the music, which is what separates the poseur from the real dancer. Second, if I could hear the structure—if I could count sets of 8—I could confirm that I was on the beat. This was sweet: I no longer had to annoy friends and accost strangers with pleas to help me with the beat. Now, if I can't count sets of 8, I know that I'm either off the beat or it's a waltz or it's not dance music.

Finally, it answered one of the more troubling aspects of dance for me as a beginner: When, exactly, do I start a dance—when do I take the first step? Let me explain. The **count 1** of any set of 8 is the best place to start a dance, because it feels like the beginning of something. While you can start a dance on any odd beat (**counts 1, 3, 5** and **7**), it will feel best if you start on a **count 1**. A **count 5,** the beginning of the second measure, is the next best choice. Generally, a follower expects you to start on a **1** or a **5**. If you don't, you may surprise her and it'll be an awkward start.

Teachers always start a class dancing on a **count 1** of the music. For now, pay attention as your teacher counts you in to start a dance. This is probably the only time you'll hear music counted and you'll usually hear just four to eight beats of it. Invariably, the teacher will start the music and then count

## Advanced Info Alert: Intro to Phrasing

**P**hrasing, the way dancers use the word, refers to the structure of the music. While phrasing is not for newbies, I believe beginners who have had a few months of classes should begin to develop an ear for it. I'll be gentle.

One set of 8 is also called a **mini-phrase,** a term coined by dance educator Skippy Blair. To the ear, a set of 8 or mini-phrase usually has a theme: a short piece of melody or harmony with a beginning and an ending. The themes of mini-phrases have some integrity, but they don't tell the whole story. A mini-phrase, like a sentence of words, only tells part of the story.

Music also has "paragraphs." A paragraph in music is often called a *phrase* of music or, more descriptively, a *major phrase.* Just as a paragraph is a series of sentences, a **major phrase** is a series of mini-phrases. To the ear, the theme of a major phrase typically encompasses the smaller themes of the mini-phrases to create a larger theme, which tells the whole story—a complete musical thought. For example, a group of mini-phrases can come together to form a chorus or verse, which is thematically complete.

Unlike the mini-phrase, which is always eight beats (except waltz music), the number of beats in a major phrase will vary depending on the music. The most common major phrase is the *32-beat phrase,* which is sometimes described as "four sets of 8" ($4 \times 8 = 32$), easy to hear in everything from jazz to Latin to rock 'n roll. Also common is the *48-beat phrase,* which can be described as "six sets of 8" and is considered standard phrasing for blues music. (*Arcane technical info:* Musicians call it *12-bar blues,* a *bar* being slang for a four-beat measure: $12 \times 4 = 48$.)

Phrasing is important, because at the intermediate level and above you will dance to the major phrases. You will choreograph step patterns in a way that acknowledges the major phrases, which will connect you to the music at a higher level. And women will love you for it.

*Freebie Video:* There are some short videos on my website that count out 32-beat phrases.

something like " . . . and a five six seven eight," and you will take your first step on the next beat, the **count 1** of the next set of 8. Any other counting a teacher does is probably counting step patterns, not the music.

I still remember the feelings of being lost, standing motionless on the floor, like a statue, waiting uncomfortably, sometimes straining to hold back the sweat, trying to discern when to start. I danced for years feeling awkward about jumping into a dance because I didn't know that virtually all dance music is structured in sets of 8 creating natural, predictable places to start. I found it interesting that teachers knew just where to start, but I figured that's why they were the teachers—they had a gift—and I was the inept student. Sure, I guess I heard sentences in the music, but I didn't know these sentences were so regular, consistent and predictable. I thought music was more random, always different. I now know this ignorance kept me from connecting to the music and stuck at the beginner level, in a rut.

Please, no tears.

# Chapter 3

# Downbeat and Upbeat

So you can't dance? Not at all? Not even one
step? How can you say that you've taken any
trouble to live when you won't even dance?

— *German-Swiss Nobel Prize-winning*
*poet and novelist Hermann Hesse*

I have a memory from childhood, from that old TV show
*Hee Haw*, of a man dressed in overalls marking time to
the music. He improvised a set of drums by alternating a stomp
of his foot with a clap of his hands. Eight beats of music went
like this: *stomp clap, stomp clap, stomp clap, stomp clap.* I now
know that this guy was capturing the *downbeat* and *upbeat*,
which is the natural pairing of beats that occurs in virtually all
dance music. The stomp was the *downbeat* and the clap was the
*upbeat.*

*I believe the downbeat and upbeat are the secret to master-*
*ing the beat of the music.* This is the pattern that got me to feel the
beat, to bring it beyond my ears and into my body. When I hear it
I know I've probably found the underlying beat (if I'm not sure I
listen for sets of 8 to confirm that I'm on the beat). When I feel it,
I believe it acts like an autopilot and keeps me on the beat.

As the *Hee Haw* musician demonstrated, it's a simple
two-beat pattern that usually comes from the drums. All dance
music—except the waltz—has this structure, albeit in the background; and it repeats with every two beats of music. The first
beat of the pair, the **downbeat**, is often, but not always, a heavier
or deeper pitched beat, as if it were created by a bass drum or
bass string instrument. The second beat, the **upbeat**, is often, but

not always, a lighter or higher pitched beat, like the sound of a snare drum or cymbals. Thus, instead of two beats sounding like *thump thump* or *tap tap*, which is how I simplistically described the underlying beat on page 24, two beats really sound more like *thump tap*. If you say it out loud, try emphasizing it like this: *thum TAA!!!*

Get a Sharpie and write this down: "The concept of two-beat increments is important." We'll keep returning to it.

Recalling that beats are numbered and come in sets of 8, when counting music the downbeats are the odd beats (**counts 1, 3, 5** and **7**) and the upbeats are the even beats (**counts 2, 4, 6** and **8**). *The first step of almost every dance occurs on a downbeat.*

As with most elements of music, the downbeat and upbeat is subtle at first. It'll be easiest to hear in songs with upbeats that are strongly accented (I give some song suggestions in a moment). The emphasis on the upbeat varies tremendously, so expect it to be obvious in some songs and elusive in others. I find that swing music and blues music generally have pronounced upbeats, which is why it's easy for me to hear the beat in those genres. Salsa, in addition to the profusion of drumming, tends to emphasize the downbeat, which makes it a bit trickier. A lot of contemporary music, especially rap, has easy-to-hear upbeats.

But regardless of the degree of emphasis on the upbeat, beats have a natural pairing, and in good dance music the second beat of the pair hits the ear differently than the first. Over time you'll see that this pairing, especially if the distinction between beats is vague, is more of a feeling than an auditory difference; it's something that's just *in* the music. If I can't identify the downbeat and upbeat it's either not dance music or it's a waltz.

After I trained my ear to hear the downbeat and upbeat combo, I was amazed at the preponderance of songs with a distinctive pairing of beats. While music websites like the iTunes Store are a great way to sample a lot of cuts (you can hear 30 seconds for free), I believe surfing the radio dial, for variety and serendipity, is a good exercise; it's sort of a test, as you need the ability to hear this structure in all types of music to be comfortable dancing to anything that may be thrown your way. However, not all music on the radio is dance music—that's part of the test.

*Lingo Alert*: I've heard other terms used to identify the downbeat and the upbeat and I've heard downbeat and upbeat used to describe other stuff. In particular, musicians use these words differently than dancers. I lament this lack of uniformity, but that's the way it is. Check with yoursource when you hear these terms used.

## EXERCISE 2: DOWNBEATS AND UPBEATS

Listen for the downbeat and upbeat structure in a variety of music. Especially listen for how the upbeat hits the ear differently than the downbeat. Choose songs with pronounced upbeats so it'll be easy to hear—*you have to hear it in the easy music before you'll be able to hear it in the hard stuff.* Do you feel the lifting feeling of the higher-pitched upbeat? Does the *thump tap* of the downbeat and upbeat create a rhythmic feeling that better defines the underlying beat? When I was learning to hear the beat I always had success with 1950s–60s oldies music: it's good dance music, especially for swing, cha-cha and rumba; tempos are slow enough to easily keep time; the sets of 8 and downbeats and upbeats are easy to hear; it's easy to find oldies stations on the radio; and the music is easy on the ears. For comparison, sample some salsa and disco (or "house") music. Salsa, as I've previously warned, often has a beat that's hard to hear; so don't dwell on that genre for now. Disco doesn't have the profusion of drumming found in salsa; so the beat is easy to hear—typically, it's a hard, driving beat, very easy to hear—but it's often hard to distinguish between the downbeat and upbeat. Disco often sounds more *thump thump* than *thump tap*, which may be one reason why some people find it monotonous. Where's my mirror ball?

## Examples of Songs with Emphasized Upbeats

Short of embedding a computer chip in the book, there's not much I can do in these pages to let you hear the downbeat and upbeat. *Freebie Video:* If you poke around my website, you'll find video clips where I identify the downbeat and upbeat using a variety of music.

I wanted to give you a list of songs in the book that have pronounced upbeats, especially songs that have clapping on the upbeat. But a song has different arrangements, performances and recordings, so the same song doesn't always sound the same; it would be hard to steer you to the exact recording that I've listened to. But it's easy to do that in the videos I've made. Plus I can visually identify the musical components. Don't expect much—a maestro I'm not.

That said, I'll mention two songs, which you can search for on, say, iTunes or YouTube. First, *Shame* by Evelyn Champagne King. This is a good place to start, as you can hear clapping on the upbeat; and I've heard the clapping on every recording of the song. Second, *Family Affair,* by Mary J. Blige. This song doesn't have clapping but it has a distinctive and typical *thum TAA,* which is what you hear in a lot of popular music. These songs are just a place to start.

## EXERCISE 3: CLAPPING AND SNAPPING

Although audiences often do it wrong, when you clap to most popular music, *you're supposed to clap on just the upbeat,* which gives a nice lifting feeling and makes the music swing a little. Most audiences will, incorrectly, clap on every beat or just the downbeat. Experiment with a variety of popular music, especially some with pronounced upbeats. Clap only on the upbeat, then only on the downbeat, then both the downbeat and upbeat. Which one feels best? It's subtle; so don't think too hard. Just relax and feel it in your body. Snapping your fingers to music works the same way—you're supposed to snap on just the upbeat. *Advanced Exercise:* Find some mellow, folksy rock music with hard-to-hear downbeats and upbeats. Repeat the experiment above, snapping your fingers instead of clapping. The beginning of the 1964 hit, *King of the Road*, by Roger Miller, is a classic example of snapping on the upbeat (you can find it on YouTube—it has to be the original recording by Roger Miller).

## EXERCISE 4: STOMP CLAP

Listening to music, try the stomp clap combo discussed earlier (stomp a foot on the downbeat, clap hands on the upbeat) and compare it to just a stomp stomp. I find the stomp clap combo fascinating. When I do it to most popular music, I almost feel like I'm an instrument jamming with the band; but if I stomp my foot on every beat, it feels like I'm just stomping my foot—I don't feel as connected to the music. I've found this stomp clap maneuver handy when faking musical talent with friends (I can't sing, so I provide the rhythm section when they sing or play a guitar).

## EXERCISE 5: BODY SQUEEZE

Let the beat inspire movement in your entire body, not just the feet. Experiment with different types of music, particularly stuff with beats that are easy to hear. Maybe turn up the bass and turn down the treble. Let the head bob and the body sway; let your whole body absorb the music. Be conscious of your solar plexus and, making small movements, try letting it move side-to-side to the beat (try tracing a bit of an arc pattern). Also, when you get a song with a pronounced upbeat, try squeezing your body a bit on the upbeat, as if there were a pulse going through your body, which would, theoretically, stretch your body and make your head rise. Try some of your favorite music too, some music that naturally moves you. Be brave: turn down the lights and let go.

Whenever you hear music—the morning commute, the elevator, watching TV—listen for the beat. Listen for sets of 8 and the downbeats and upbeats until they are second nature. Know the beat well.

# PART 2

# Rhythm

# Chapter 4

# *Rhythm Patterns*

I actually think, to be a complete person
I should know how to dance.

— *Kurt Inderbitzin, movie producer,*
*The Learning Channel's* Ballroom Bootcamp

Forget what you know about the word *rhythm*. Forget the dictionary definitions too. Forget, especially, what you think you know about rhythm in relation to music; that's a different book, a book on music. Prepare to learn about rhythm in relation to dance. Enter the world of *rhythm patterns*.

For me, grasping the concept of a rhythm pattern was profound. Finally, I was in control. The dance floor, once a morass that held me at bay, now seduced me. But I couldn't have discovered the splendor of rhythm without time spent stumbling through some steps. It's a process. Stumble on.

While there's a long list of items that must come together to perform a new move, for the beginner, the two most important are *rhythm pattern* and *direction*. I don't think I'm sticking my neck out if I say that when they teach step patterns, teachers focus on direction, which is *where* your feet go. You put your left foot here . . . you put your right foot there . . . and so on.

Yeah, yeah, all those twists, tucks and turns are smart-looking, but I believe the rhythm pattern, which tells your feet *when* to go, when to make weight changes, is what beginners should focus on first. After an eternity of missteps, stumbles and stomping on toes, I came to realize that *when first learning a dance and, especially, for gaining an understanding of dance in general, the rhythm pattern (when to step) is more important than the direction (where to step) because it's what connects you to the music.* But the direction is important too, so all I'm really saying about learning a new step is this: first nail down the rhythm pattern, which can be practiced by stepping in place, before you wear yourself out moving around the floor.

Before you can grasp rhythm patterns, you need to learn about *dance rhythms.* (It can be a little confusing because *dance rhythm* sounds like *rhythm pattern,* and *rhythm pattern* is close to *step pattern.* Put a bookmark on these terms in the glossary at the back of the book for reference.) Dance rhythms are the foundation of rhythm patterns and are the most important concept in this book. In the world of dance, dance rhythms are right up there with gravity and the world is round. Let me explain.

When you dance, some beats of music receive a weight change and some don't. When talking about weight changes, wouldn't it be neat if there were a concise language to identify, discuss and remember different patterns? For example, wouldn't it be nice if there were simple words to describe the difference between these three, eight-beat patterns:

| **PATTERN 1** | STEP | STEP | STEP | STEP | STEP | STEP | STEP | STEP |
|---|---|---|---|---|---|---|---|---|
| **PATTERN 2** | STEP | TOUCH | STEP | TOUCH | STEP | TOUCH | STEP | TOUCH |
| **PATTERN 3** | STEP | STEP | STEP | TOUCH | STEP | STEP | STEP | TOUCH |

*Note:* A TOUCH represents a beat of music with no weight change.

Thanks to dance educator Skippy Blair, there is. Although most step patterns are six or eight beats long, Skippy discovered that it's easiest to learn a new dance step if you break it into two-beat increments, which she calls *dance rhythms* (also known as *rhythm units*). So a **dance rhythm** is the number of weight changes in two beats of music (except waltz, see pages 74 and 124). When you string dance rhythms together to create a step pattern, Skippy calls it a **rhythm pattern**, which is a combination of two or more dance rhythms.

Meditate for a moment on the concept of two-beat dance

## The Einstein of Rhythm: Skippy Blair

It was through the genius of Skippy Blair that I learned the importance of dance rhythms. As simple as it sounds, it was Skippy who discovered that two beats of music is the smallest size that establishes an identifiable, danceable, repeatable dance rhythm. Her system of rhythm and dance, Dance Dynamics and the Universal Unit System, which is beyond the scope of this book, was first introduced in her classic 1978 book, *Skippy Blair on Contemporary Social Dance: Disco to Tango and Back*. You can contact her and her organization, Golden State Dance Teachers Association (GSDTA), for more information: (562) 869-8949 or swingworld.com.

*Where Credit Is Due:* All of the specific dance rhythms discussed in this chapter are terms Skippy Blair has coined:

*single rhythm, double rhythm, triple rhythm, syncopated triple rhythm, delayed single rhythm* and *blank rhythm*. While it's beyond the scope of this book, she has discovered over 25 dance rhythms that are the building blocks for all the patterns of every social dance. But most are more advanced syncopations, which involve stepping between the beats of the music.

*Disclaimer:* Skippy helped me go from a rhythmically-challenged-bad-beginner—who knew some intermediate patterns so I thought I was an intermediate dancer—to a competent and confident social dancer. But, for the record, this book does not represent Skippy Blair's system of dance. While I've trained with her for years, this book simply uses some of her terminology and reflects my experience using some of the elementary parts of her system.

rhythms. You learned in Chapter 3, "Downbeat and Upbeat," that dance beats come in pairs, a downbeat followed by an upbeat, so the notion of two-beat increments should already make some sense. Dance rhythms give structure to dance; just as words are the building blocks of sentences, two-beat dance rhythms are the building blocks of longer rhythm patterns. Imagine how difficult it would be to read a sentence if youdidnotseparatethewords.

Worse, imagine how difficult it would be ify ousepa ratedt hewo rdsint hewro ngpla ces.

There are only two dance rhythms of great importance to the beginning survival dancer, *single rhythm* and *double rhythm*; and there's a third, *triple rhythm*, which rounds out the set. To identify these dance rhythms, simply ask, how many steps are taken in two beats of music? If one step is taken it's called **single rhythm**. If two steps are taken it's **double rhythm**. And, no surprise, three weight changes in two beats of music is **triple rhythm**. I love single, double and triple rhythm because they're so darn logical. Now look at the same three patterns, broken into two-beat dance rhythms:

| PATTERN 1 | STEP STEP | STEP STEP | STEP STEP | STEP STEP |
|---|---|---|---|---|
| RHYTHM PATTERN | *double* | *double* | *double* | *double* |

| PATTERN 2 | STEP TOUCH | STEP TOUCH | STEP TOUCH | STEP TOUCH |
|---|---|---|---|---|
| RHYTHM PATTERN | *single* | *single* | *single* | *single* |

| PATTERN 3 | STEP STEP | STEP TOUCH | STEP STEP | STEP TOUCH |
|---|---|---|---|---|
| RHYTHM PATTERN | *double* | *single* | *double* | *single* |

Identifying dance rhythms makes learning and remembering any new step pattern easy. Not only can the sequence of weight changes be easily communicated and remembered, such as *double—double—double—double* for Pattern 1, or *double—single—double—single* for Pattern 3; but if a teacher in class said the rhythm pattern to a new move is *double—single—single,* or *double—triple—triple,* you'd have a head start in learning the pattern. You would know immediately on what beats there are weight changes, something that, in my experience, is not always communicated well in dance classes.

For me, dance rhythm was the key that unlocked the door to dance. I believe the secret to understanding dance is this: *almost every basic step pattern of a dance is some combination of single, double and triple rhythm.* That's right, almost any new step you learn in a beginners' class, if broken into two-beat increments, will be a combination of these three simple dance rhythms.

As a beginner, and for basic survival on the dance floor, you'll mostly use just single and double rhythm, which is the focus of this book. In fact, the foundation of improvising dance, including slow dancing, is simply the ability to mix single and double rhythm. Triple rhythm, which involves a step between two beats of music, is harder to do, but it's good to know, especially if you want to do any of the swing dances. Let's dig a little into each dance rhythm but, first, an important Lingo Alert on how teachers communicate patterns to students using a *verbal call.*

*Lingo Alert:* When you learn a step pattern in class, teachers call out the pattern by using words, spoken over the music, as you dance. Often these **verbal calls** establish the timing for an action, like when to step (in this book, verbal calls are all capitalized). They often give direction (for example, FORWARD, BACK, SIDE) or an action (for example, STEP, KICK), which can help you to remember what to do. You'll see more examples in a moment. But be prepared: Teachers have numerous ways—some logical and some not—to call a dance. Some teachers follow this school of dance, some follow that school of dance and some follow their own school of dance. And be prepared for teachers to use a combination of methods to describe the same pattern. *Caution:* The misunderstanding of how step patterns are called can stunt your growth, so ask questions it you're not sure. I found some calls downright confusing. In particular, numbers perplexed me for a long time. Chapter 6, "Counting Step Patterns," sets the record straight on using numbers to count step patterns.

**Single rhythm** is one weight change in two beats of music. You take a step on the first beat (the downbeat), but you do not step on the second beat (the upbeat). For now, to label the upbeat we'll use the word TOUCH, which is an action without a weight change (you can touch your toe to the floor, but without shifting your weight). So, for the moment, we'll verbally call single rhythm STEP TOUCH. But there are other ways to call it that depend upon the specific actions and the teacher's preference.

For example, in addition to STEP, other common words you might hear to describe a weight change include WALK, CHECK, BREAK, LEFT, RIGHT, FORWARD, BACK and SIDE. The list could be endless; it's whatever a teacher wants to use. In addition to TOUCH, other examples of words without a weight change include POINT, KICK, SWEEP, DRAG, TAP, HOLD and FREEZE. To stay connected to the beat, when there's no weight change on a beat of music you should still put in an action word, or a non-action word to describe a pose, such as HOLD or FREEZE. The word SLOW, a common call for single rhythm, is an example of a call that does not account for the second beat of music, which can cause a problem.

Let's look at the eight-beat rhythm pattern that uses all single rhythm, *single—single—single—single.* I'm including the musical count too, because you need to get used to seeing numbers. It looks like this:

## ALL SINGLE RHYTHM

| MUSICAL COUNT | 1 | 2 | 3 | 4 | 5 | 6 | 7 | 8 |
|---|---|---|---|---|---|---|---|---|
| VERBAL CALL | STEP | TOUCH | STEP | TOUCH | STEP | TOUCH | STEP | TOUCH |
| RHYTHM PATTERN | *single* | | *single* | | *single* | | *single* | |

People who can't dance often appear to be doing single rhythm, but if they're not connected to the music (that is, if they're not stepping on the beat), they just end up slowly rocking back and forth, off time. Nonetheless, people attempt single rhythm when they can't dance because it involves the fewest number of steps yet still has some semblance of being a dance. Dancing single rhythm on time is something every beginner should be comfortable doing. If this rhythm pattern is new to you, the box on page 64, "How to Mark Single Rhythm," will get you started. There's more on using single rhythm to survive on the dance floor in Chapter 13, "Survival Dancing."

## QUICKs and SLOWs

If you've had any dance lessons, you've probably heard the verbal calls of QUICK and SLOW, labels first introduced by Arthur Murray back in the 1950s. A SLOW is just a single rhythm and a QUICK QUICK—I go by the rule that QUICKs should always come in pairs—is just a double rhythm. I'm not endorsing the use of QUICKs and SLOWs; in fact, while I find them convenient, they caused a problem for me. If you struggle hearing the beat, the use of SLOW as a verbal call can make it hard to keep track of the beat (because it does not account for the upbeat).

**TIP** If you hear QUICKs and SLOWs used, have your teacher clarify how many beats of music each represents and, specifically, on what syllables you should make weight changes.

**Double rhythm** is two weight changes in two beats of music. You take a step on the first beat and another step on the second beat. One way to verbally call double rhythm is STEP STEP, although there are many ways to call double rhythm depending upon the teacher. Let's look at the eight-beat rhythm pattern that repeats double rhythm, *double—double—double double:*

## ALL DOUBLE RHYTHM

| MUSICAL COUNT | 1 | 2 | 3 | 4 | 5 | 6 | 7 | 8 |
|---|---|---|---|---|---|---|---|---|
| VERBAL CALL | STEP | STEP | STEP | STEP | STEP | STEP | STEP | STEP |
| RHYTHM PATTERN | *double* | | *double* | | *double* | | *double* | |

Dancing all double rhythm is another rhythm pattern you should be comfortable doing. This rhythm pattern is sometimes used when improvising steps to unfamiliar music, particularly slower tempos, because it's the familiar rhythm pattern used in walking. It's sometimes referred to as a *walking rhythm* or a *marching rhythm*, although it won't necessarily look like a walk when danced. There is one dance that uses this rhythm, the merengue, one of the Latin dances. But most dancing departs from the metronome-like rhythm pattern created by stepping on every beat. Fancy footwork is part of the skill and thrill of dancing.

**Triple rhythm** is three weight changes in two beats of music. So far, all steps have been made on a beat of music; triple rhythm, in a simple but exciting way, departs from this protocol. In addition to a step on a downbeat and an upbeat, there's also a step between those two beats of music on what's known as the **&** or, as it's often labeled, the **& count**. The freedom to step between beats, on that little **& count**, creates many new possibilities known as *syncopations*. Some common verbal calls for triple rhythm include: STEP-THREE-TIMES and TRI-PLE-STEP. There's more on the **& count**, a concept I struggled with, in Chapter 6, "Counting Step Patterns." (*Lingo Alert:* The concept of syncopation in dance steps is different than syncopation in music.)

In addition to defining the look of swing, there are several dances that are composed entirely of triple rhythm: samba, nightclub two-step and polka. Let's look at the eight-beat rhythm pattern that uses all triple rhythm, *triple—triple—triple—triple*:

## ALL TRIPLE RHYTHM

| MUSICAL COUNT | 1 | 2 | | 3 | 4 | | 5 | 6 | | 7 | 8 |
|---|---|---|---|---|---|---|---|---|---|---|---|
| VERBAL CALL | STEP-THREE-TIMES | | | STEP-THREE-TIMES | | | STEP-THREE-TIMES | | | STEP-THREE-TIMES | |
| RHYTHM PATTERN | *triple* | | | *triple* | | | *triple* | | | *triple* | |

Triple rhythm is difficult compared to single and double rhythm. Here are three reasons why triple rhythm eluded me for a long time:

- I had a hard time grasping the concept of stepping between two beats of music because I had trouble finding the beat.

- I didn't realize that dancing a triple (three steps), takes the same amount of time (two beats of music) as dancing a double (two steps), *so it requires your feet to move faster.* Part of the problem was, in class, I didn't grasp the pace that my teachers mouthed the verbal calls; I didn't realize that when I heard the call of a triple rhythm, STEP-THREE-TIMES, that the words were coming out faster than the call of the double rhythm, STEP STEP.

- Finally, triples require more technique than singles and doubles. Unlike singles and doubles, the body movement to execute a triple is not a natural walking step. See the box on page 67 for more technique.

**ADVANCED INFO ALERT** You just learned that single, double and triple rhythms are the building blocks that create the basic step patterns of almost all the dances. For perspective, I'll quickly run through the exceptions. First, there's *blank rhythm*, used in American tango, which is no weight changes in two beats of music. In the tango, I verbally call that dance rhythm, DRAG TAP, two actions with no weight changes. I love the blank rhythm, as it's used in dips, and I use it a lot when improvising footwork. Second, there's the *delayed single rhythm* used in mambo and Balboa, which is one weight change in two beats, but the step occurs on the second beat, the upbeat, which creates a TOUCH STEP (*Note:* that's different from single rhythm—STEP TOUCH—which you learned earlier). Third, there's the *syncopated triple rhythm* used in cha-cha and hustle, but there's no easy way to describe it until you learn how to count patterns in Chapter 6, "Counting Step Patterns" (all right already: a triple is danced **1&2**, but a syncopated triple is danced **&1 2**—still three steps in two beats of music, but it has a different look). Finally, there's the waltz, which I've been telling you is the exception to all the rules. Waltz uses two three-beat dance rhythms to create a set of 6 (pages 74 and 124).

*continued on page 58*

## Rhythm Patterns for Common Social Dances

These rhythm patterns are for the basic step patterns of each dance, the primary pattern that defines the look of the dance (this list is subjective; see my disclaimer that follows). For five of the most popular dances—salsa, rumba, foxtrot, swing and waltz—you can see the rhythm pattern in relation to a verbal call and the pattern count in Chapter 6, "Counting Step Patterns" (salsa, rumba, page 69; foxtrot, page 70; swing, page 72; waltz, page 74).

*Note:* All patterns are eight beats unless otherwise noted (but you should see that without my help because each dance rhythm, except waltz, is two beats of music).

**salsa:** *double—single—double—single*

**mambo:** *delayed single—double—delayed single—double*

**rumba:** *double—single—double—single* (see the next Advanced Info Alert for a variation)

**cha-cha ("on two"):** *syncopated triple—double—syncopated triple—double* (this is the formal cha-cha taught in studios)

**cha-cha ("on one"):** *double—triple—double—triple* (the colloquial cha-cha, which is used in less formal situations)

**merengue:** *double—double* (a four-beat rhythm pattern)

**samba:** *triple—triple* (a four-beat rhythm pattern)

**East Coast swing:** *double—triple—triple* (a six-beat rhythm pattern; see the next Advanced Info Alert for a variation; I also call this dance the *jitterbug;* an option for up-tempo music or if you can't dance triple rhythm is to do a "single rhythm East Coast swing," which is far fewer steps and goes like this: *double—single—single*)

**West Coast swing:** *double—triple—triple* (a six-beat rhythm pattern)

**Lindy Hop:** *double—triple—double—triple*

**Balboa:** *double—delayed single—double—delayed single*

**Carolina shag:** *double—triple—triple* (a six-beat rhythm pattern)

**hustle:** *double—syncopated triple—triple* (a six-beat rhythm pattern)

**nightclub two-step:** *triple—triple* (a four-beat rhythm pattern)

**foxtrot:** *double—single—single* (a six-beat rhythm pattern; see the next Advanced Info Alert for a variation)

**American tango:** *single—single—double—blank* (SLOW—
SLOW—QUICK QUICK—SLOW is a common verbal call,
but note that the last SLOW is really a blank rhythm, not a
single rhythm like the first two SLOWs)

**Argentine tango:** either all singles or all doubles or a mix of
singles and doubles (many styles exist, so there's not a
standard basic pattern)

**country two-step:** *double—single—single* (a six-beat rhythm
pattern; see the next Advanced Info Alert for a variation)

**polka:** *triple—triple* (a four-beat rhythm pattern)

**waltz:** *triple—triple* (a six-beat rhythm pattern; the three-beat
waltz triple, different from the two-beat triples used in all
other dances, is explained on page 74)

*Disclaimer:* This is not a complete list, it's just my list. There's an abundance of dance styles, variations and opinions, so no list would satisfy everyone. In fact, not everyone will think this list is accurate. Fine, don't sweat it; if a dance is presented differently, just figure out what counts get weight changes and adjust (see the next Advanced Info Alert). Thinking about rhythm in two-beat increments will make adjusting easy. Flexibility will make you a more desirable partner.

**ADVANCED INFO ALERT** In some dances, a teacher or partner may use a different arrangement of dance rhythms. Rumba, which is *double—single—double—single,* is sometimes danced *single—double—single—double.* Likewise, the foxtrot and country two-step, *double—single—single,* are sometimes danced *single—single—double.* And swing, *double—triple—triple,* is often danced *triple—triple—double.* There are different ways to teach dance, so it's important to remain flexible enough to dance rhythm patterns any which way a teacher or partner might request. Don't fret, just dance; it'll probably work out fine. If you think about patterns in two-beat rhythm increments, rearrangements and substitutions—such as replacing the triples with singles in East Coast swing when the tempo gets too fast—become much easier. Ambiguities in dance exist, and it's best to blend, not resist. Be the Bruce Lee of dance and learn to block and parry the idiosyncrasies of the art.

For most people, and especially for the struggling beginner, focusing on rhythm is a powerful tool. In class, I used to get overwhelmed by verbal calls that I didn't understand, like "rock–step–triple–step–kick–ball–change." I was bombarded with stuff like that and nothing made sense until I understood the underlying rhythm pattern and when to make weight changes. When I am first learning a new step pattern, if the teacher doesn't identify the rhythm pattern, I do these five steps (on page 73, I add a final sixth step to this list):

**1.** I listen for the downbeat and upbeat and sets of 8 to make sure I'm on the beat and connected to the music.

**2.** If the teacher doesn't announce it, I figure out how many beats are in the step pattern, which is usually six or eight (sometimes four).

**3.** I note which beats have weight changes, which beats have no weight changes and if there are any steps between beats of music. If I'm confused, this is when I ask the teacher questions, which are usually related to understanding the verbal call being used and when to make weight changes. (For example, if I didn't understand the call, "kick–ball–change," I might ask, "Is there a weight change on the 'ball'?")

**4.** I identify the two-beat dance rhythms, which will be mostly single, double and triple rhythm.

**5.** I string the dance rhythms together to identify the rhythm pattern (for example, *double—single—double—single*) so the pattern will be easier to remember and to see how similar it is to other steps that I know.

I then burn the rhythm pattern into my brain by *marking* it in place (see Chapter 5, "Marking Rhythms"). I start in class the moment I identify the pattern. Between songs and as the teacher talks, I nonchalantly mark the rhythm in place, verbally calling it to myself. At the end of class I review the rhythm pattern before I leave; if I'm not sure of it, I ask questions. On the ride home I review it in my head. At home, I practice it over and over until I can do it without thinking.

Practicing just the rhythm pattern is much easier than

trying to do the entire step pattern (rhythm pattern and direction) all at once. Behold the beauty of practicing just the rhythm pattern: there aren't many body parts to move so it's relatively effortless; you can do it by yourself so there's no partner to step on and annoy; and you can do it away from the dance floor. Once you know the rhythm pattern to a new step and are free from that demand, laying on the other elements, like the direction, the lead and follow and the styling, will be easier.

Getting familiar with different rhythms patterns, on my own, is what allowed me to overcome my clumsiness and anxiety on the floor. I was relentless when it came to learning rhythm patterns, and I did it everywhere, whether I was sitting out a dance, at the gym, in line at the post office, waiting for a web page to load or drifting off to sleep at night. Chapter 5, "Marking Rhythms," will take you into that process.

Getting familiar with rhythm patterns also led to a minor revelation that expanded my capacity to quickly learn new steps: *two (or more) completely different dances can have the same rhythm pattern.* For example, *double—single—double—single* is shared between salsa and rumba. Huh . . . I mean, how can two different dances have the same rhythm pattern? Rhythm patterns alone do not define the dance since they do not tell us what direction to move. In addition to rhythm pattern and direction, styling and music play a part in defining a dance. I found that by identifying the similarities between dances—and there are many—you can use your experience in one dance to learn another.

While developing muscle memory for different rhythm patterns takes time, there are only a few a guy needs to know to survive. In fact, there are very few situations that one of these three patterns can't handle, which happen to be patterns 1, 2 and 3 from earlier in this chapter:

1. *single—single—single—single* (all single rhythm)

2. *double—double—double—double* (all double rhythm)

3. *double—single—double—single* (the salsa–rumba rhythm pattern)

These three patterns are all you need to know to save face on the floor. Your wedding dance? Done. A dance you don't know at a friend's wedding? No problem. Lounge dancing? Nailed. Country and western bar? Affirmative. Big band at a banquet or a ball? Have at it. Latin combo? You betcha. Slow dance? Sign me up. Blues band? Somebody stop me. Welcome dance on the space shuttle? Bring it on!

Does this mean you just need to learn these three rhythm patterns and don't need to take lessons? Not so fast—you should take lessons in at least one dance so you can learn partnering skills, especially how to lead. But it's hard, as well as time consuming, to learn a lot of dances—only a teacher or some sort of dance geek would learn them all. Besides, they'll quickly be forgotten if you don't practice each dance on a regular basis. If you have a sincere interest in learning to dance but limited time, I suggest you get good at one dance and then learn just the basic step pattern for some of the others. As the years pass, you'll naturally get better at the dances you do more often.

Don your dancing shoes . . . and away we go.

# Chapter 5

# Marking Rhythms

In order to be a good soldier it is
necessary to know how to dance.
— *Plato*

Getting the hang of music and rhythm will take time: there is no *Learn the Beat in 60 Seconds*, there is no *Five Easy Steps to Hearing Sets of 8* and there is no *Three Minutes to Better Rhythm*. Thankfully, practicing is easy. You can do it anywhere, without a partner—heck, you can do it lying poolside, with a cold drink in hand, listening to an iPod.

It's time to get cozy with rhythm patterns, time to burn them deep into your primordial brain.

Learning rhythm patterns is straightforward, but it takes a lot of repetition to reach the point where you can thoughtlessly execute a variety of patterns. Thoughtless execution, the ability to do it without thinking, is the goal. When dancing, you need to focus on other things, like the direction of movement, adjusting to your partner, the lead and follow, what step pattern to do next, navigating through traffic and, if you're like me, keeping your cool.

The best way to learn a new rhythm pattern is to *mark* it, a technique you should do when first learning a new step pattern. The best way to **mark** a rhythm is to do weight changes while standing in place. This is something you do before you move around the floor, even before you touch your partner.

Taking it a step further, the best way to learn rhythm patterns in general is to mark a variety of them—say, the most common ones used in dance—until they become second nature. This is not something you will do in class but it's something you can do on your own, at home, alone. In this chapter we'll focus on the three rhythm patterns you need to know to survive:

- All single rhythm

- All double rhythm

- The salsa-rumba rhythm pattern

Once you can find the beat, I believe marking rhythm patterns is the most important, most valuable, most indispensable tool for the beginner, especially if learning to dance is a struggle. This is what I used to lift myself from rhythmically challenged to dance bliss.

To get started, all you need is some danceable music and a patch of floor. Carpet will do. You can do this barefoot, in Birkenstocks or in Bruno Maglis. Stand in place, weight on the right foot for the men (left foot for the women). Then mark the different rhythm patterns by doing weight changes in place. *For men, the first step in a dance is almost always with your left foot.* As you step, call the rhythm patterns, either aloud or silently in your head, using the words STEP for a weight change and TOUCH for a beat of music with no weight change. On the TOUCH, *touch* your unweighted toe to the floor; this gives you an action to do precisely on the beat, to help your timing.

Mark the rhythm patterns to a variety of music, particularly to a range of tempos; but keep it slow when you start. Pay attention to tempos, and note the tempo range where a rhythm pattern works best. It'll be easiest if you choose music with strongly accented upbeats. Start on any **count 1** of the music, the first beat of a set of 8, so you will be better connected to the music. If you're still struggling to hear the sets of 8, use songs that you're sure of.

You don't need a big collection of dance music. If you like, just surf the radio dial; easy rock, jazz and oldies stations are good places to start. If a piece of music stumps you—too fast, can't hear the beat—move quickly to another station, as you have to do it to the easy music before you can handle the hard stuff. Over time, practice to a variety of musical genres to sharpen your skill and to gain the confidence that you can dance to any kind of music.

For many months, marking rhythm patterns with actual weight changes was a part of my daily routine in life. Depending upon your aptitude and how much you practice, you may spend days, weeks or months on one rhythm pattern before it is indelibly and irrevocably tattooed on your brain.

**TIP** It was exciting to rhythm-train my body, and I got creative in marking patterns. If I was seated and didn't want to stand, I would, using both feet to simulate dancing, do simple taps on the floor instead of doing weight changes. If I was lying down I would tap the air, again using both feet as if I were dancing. If my feet weren't available, I'd tap my two index fingers. Sometimes I'd shift my solar plexus from side to side, as if I were doing weight changes. Sometimes I'd bob my head from side to side, pretending they were weight changes. My goal was to get some physical movement to create muscle memory. But guess what. I could also do it motionless by just visualizing steps in my head as I listened to music (never underestimate my laziness when it comes to dance). It all helped my rhythm, timing and connection to the music.

## EXERCISE 6: MARK SINGLE RHYTHM

If you've never done single rhythm before, expect some awkwardness until you get the hang of the timing. The box titled "How to Mark Single Rhythm" will get you started. I wish I had worked out the awkwardness at home, alone, so I didn't look like a doofus in class. Mark *single—single—single—single:*

| MUSICAL COUNT | 1 | 2 | 3 | 4 | 5 | 6 | 7 | 8 |
|---|---|---|---|---|---|---|---|---|
| VERBAL CALL | STEP | TOUCH | STEP | TOUCH | STEP | TOUCH | STEP | TOUCH |
| RHYTHM PATTERN | *single* | | *single* | | *single* | | *single* | |

## How to Mark Single Rhythm

This demonstration will get you started with single rhythm by using the verbal call STEP TOUCH. I like to use TOUCH for the beat that gets no weight change, as touching the floor with your toe gives you something easy to do on the beat of music and, visually, you can make it look nice.

Start with no music, establishing your own comfortable, internal tempo. Then do it to music with a tempo that's slow enough to comfortably keep time. For now, we're making this an eight-beat step pattern, which will help you to connect to the sets of 8. When you do it to music, the tricky part is making the first step on a **count 1** of the music. When you start on a **count 1**, the step pattern will be aligned or *phrased* to the music. It'll take time to get this right—to get on the **1**—and your success will vary from song to song. Expect some frustration.

Stand with your weight on the right foot. Now, stepping in place, mark four single rhythms. Then repeat. The key moves in this exercise are on the beats with no weight change, the upbeats (**2, 4, 6** and **8**): just touch your toe to the floor. It'll help if you call the rhythm pattern out loud: STEP TOUCH—STEP TOUCH—STEP TOUCH—STEP TOUCH. And away we go . . .

> On **count 1** of the music: Transfer weight to the left foot (STEP).
>
> On **count 2**: Touch your right toe to the floor (TOUCH), with no weight change (weight remains on left foot).
>
> On **count 3**: Transfer weight to the right foot (STEP).
>
> On **count 4**: Touch your left toe to the floor (TOUCH).
>
> On **count 5**: Transfer weight to the left foot (STEP).
>
> On **count 6**: Touch your right toe to the floor (TOUCH).
>
> On **count 7**: Transfer weight to the right foot (STEP).
>
> On **count 8**: Touch your left toe to the floor (TOUCH).

Single rhythm is, essentially, stepping on every other beat of music. It has a feel to it that's different from stepping on every beat of music (all double rhythm). The point of practicing, of doing endless repetition, is to learn how the different rhythm patterns feel. Then they become second nature.

*Freebie Video:* Check out my website for a quick demo.

## EXERCISE 7: MARK DOUBLE RHYTHM

Repeating double rhythm is just a step on every beat, like a march. Mark *double—double—double—double:*

| MUSICAL COUNT | 1 | 2 | 3 | 4 | 5 | 6 | 7 | 8 |
|---|---|---|---|---|---|---|---|---|
| VERBAL CALL | STEP | STEP | STEP | STEP | STEP | STEP | STEP | STEP |
| RHYTHM PATTERN | *double* | | *double* | | *double* | | *double* | |

## EXERCISE 8: MARK DOUBLE—SINGLE—DOUBLE—SINGLE

In addition to being a great pattern for survival dancing, this is also the rhythm pattern for the basic step in both salsa and rumba:

| MUSICAL COUNT | 1 | 2 | 3 | 4 | 5 | 6 | 7 | 8 |
|---|---|---|---|---|---|---|---|---|
| VERBAL CALL | STEP | STEP | STEP | TOUCH | STEP | STEP | STEP | TOUCH |
| RHYTHM PATTERN | *double* | | *single* | | *double* | | *single* | |

Note that you're not actually doing the salsa or rumba, you're just doing the rhythm pattern that you would use to do those dances. Feel free to match some salsa music to this pattern (*Warning:* The tempo for salsa music is fast and the beat is hard to hear, so it's best to start with something slower.) Try a range of music, both in tempo and genre, and note how the salsa rhythm pattern works with a lot of different music.

TIP To train for distractions I used to read aloud from a magazine while attempting to sustain different rhythms. One of my early goals—the milestone that would prove I could thoughtlessly execute a rhythm pattern—was the ability to talk and dance at the same time. When I could dance and converse with my partner and not lose the beat or the rhythm pattern, I began to relax on the floor and excel as a dancer. Test yourself with each rhythm pattern by attempting to talk or read aloud.

## EXERCISE 9: IMPROVISE RHYTHMS

If you want to eventually be an improvisational dancer, especially a competent slow dancer—and what guy doesn't—try this variation: Take a few deep breaths, relax and see if you can make up your own rhythm patterns using just single and double rhythm. Listen to the melody of the music and see if it suggests a rhythm pattern for your feet. Improvise a little. *Advanced Exercise:* Try some dramatic pauses. When you're ready, and when the music suggests, such as when the melody slows down or resolves thematically, try adding some dramatic pauses by freezing your movement for, say, two to four beats, maybe six beats. This would be done with blank rhythm, first discussed in the Advanced Info Alert on page 55 (see also page 123). For now, verbally call a blank rhythm, HOLD HOLD. Resume stepping again on the next **count 1** of the music. In dance, your feet don't have to be constantly moving as long as you know where you are in the music. In the context of survival dancing, when it comes to making weight changes, my strategy is economy of movement. I prefer simpler styling moves, for example, creating a nice line with my body, versus complicated footwork.

After I realized the importance of rhythm patterns, whenever I learned a new pattern in class, especially harder rhythm patterns with syncopations, I'd go home and mark it until it was burned into my psyche. I did it immediately; for me, the half-life of a move from class can be as little as five minutes. Eventually I'd add the direction to the rhythm pattern. At that point, if you throw up your arms into the standard closed ballroom position

## Advanced Info Alert: Marking Triple Rhythm

| MUSICAL COUNT | 1 | 2 | | 3 | 4 | | 5 | 6 | | 7 | 8 |
|---|---|---|---|---|---|---|---|---|---|---|---|
| PATTERN COUNT | 1 | & | 2 | 3 | & | 4 | 5 | & | 6 | 7 | & | 8 |
| VERBAL CALL | STEP-THREE-TIMES | | | STEP-THREE-TIMES | | | STEP-THREE-TIMES | | | STEP-THREE-TIMES | | |
| RHYTHM PATTERN | *triple* | | | *triple* | | | *triple* | | | *triple* | | |

You don't need to know triple rhythm for basic survival on the dance floor so this is not something you need to work on unless you're taking lessons in a dance that uses triples, like swing. Triple rhythm is tricky compared to single and double rhythm so, if you're having trouble, it would be best to come back to it after reading Chapter 6, "Counting Step Patterns," which explains the **& count**.

Make certain to use music with a slow, comfortable tempo and try marking *triple—triple—triple—triple*.

Here's some technique for making triple rhythm look sharp:

• Keep your solar plexus over your left foot for the entire first triple, **1&2**. For the next triple, shift your solar plexus to the right and keep it there for the entire second triple, **3&4**. Shift weight back to the left for **5&6**, then back to the right for **7&8**. Keep your shoulders horizontal (parallel to the floor) at all times. *Double-Secret-Advanced-Info Alert:* Shift your solar plexus on the **& counts** before beats **1**, **3**, **5** and **7**.

• Instead of the verbal call, STEP–THREE–TIMES, hang back a little with the middle step by calling it like this, STEP–then–STEP–STEP, where there is no weight change on the *then*. This will get you into the pocket of the music and put a swing in your step.

(Chapter 8, "Positions"), you'd be *shadow dancing*, a great tool for training on your own. Marking rhythm patterns got me on the path to learning to dance. It was magic for my feet.

# Chapter 6

# Counting Step Patterns

Dancing is an amazing activity. You can go up to
a gorgeous woman that you've never met before,
spend three minutes touching her virtually anywhere
on her body, and she thanks you for it afterwards!

— *Swing dance instructor Mario Robau, Jr.*

Many folks have a fear of numbers and will become unnerved at the thought of counting step patterns; no doubt millions will panic. But my true grasp of dance did not occur until I learned how to count.

It's no longer a mystery why counting took so long to get. First, counting a step pattern is based on the musical beat. So when I couldn't hear the beat or count the music, the pattern count was meaningless. Not knowing any better, I accepted the unknown as something bigger than me. I explained my ineptitude by thinking, *well, they all have talent and I don't.*

Second, while I didn't know it at the time, there's more than one method of counting patterns; and the overlap of conflicting methods completely drained the logic from the process (see the box at the end of this chapter, "Counting Beats versus Counting Steps"). Boy oh boy, my brain was twisted in knots for years (I still have scar tissue). I'll warn you: I may have to vent (smoke is already coming out of my ears). Children and small animals should be sequestered.

Uh-oh, I feel the non-counters, those who shun counting patterns, becoming restless. All right already, I promise: you don't have to learn how to count to dance. While I stress counting, as

I believe it's a language every dancer should know, many people turn into good social dancers yet remain oblivious to the count. My sense is that those who don't need the count have natural ability, or else they tend to be followers who rely on their leaders for timing clues. Those who don't count develop an intuitive feel for the music and, as you learned in Chapter 4, "Rhythm Patterns," use words like STEP and TOUCH instead of numbers when verbally describing or calling patterns.

Counting, not counting—holy Einstein-versus-Beethoven, what's a newbie to do? I urge you to learn how to count step patterns.

Recall from Chapter 2, "Counting Music: Finding the Sets of 8," that counting music is counting the underlying beat in sets of 8. Counting music pertains only to the music; and virtually all dance music is counted the same, irrespective of the figure being executed. *Counting a step pattern*, which creates the **pattern count**, means identifying the sequence of weight changes in a dance figure by counting only the beats that have weight changes. Counting patterns—generally just referred to as *counting* or the *count*—pertains directly to the dance figure being danced, which changes throughout the song.

For example, *double—single—double—single,* the rhythm pattern for salsa and rumba, does not step on the **count 4** or the **count 8** of the music; so the pattern count looks like this (I've included a verbal call and the rhythm pattern to put everything in perspective):

## SALSA–RUMBA

| MUSICAL COUNT | 1 | 2 | 3 | 4 | 5 | 6 | 7 | 8 |
|---|---|---|---|---|---|---|---|---|
| PATTERN COUNT | 1 | 2 | 3 | hold-4 | 5 | 6 | 7 | hold-8 |
| VERBAL CALL | STEP | STEP | STEP | TOUCH | STEP | STEP | STEP | TOUCH |
| RHYTHM PATTERN | *double* | | *single* | | *double* | | *single* | |

Let's try another. Here's the pattern count for the foxtrot, *double—single—single:*

# FOXTROT

| | MUSICAL COUNT | 1 | 2 | 3 | 4 | 5 | 6 |
|---|---|---|---|---|---|---|---|
| PATTERN COUNT | | 1 | 2 | 3 | hold-4 | 5 | hold-6 |
| VERBAL CALL | | STEP | STEP | STEP | HOLD | STEP | HOLD |
| RHYTHM PATTERN | | *double* | | *single* | | *single* | |

It's really that simple . . . well, not so fast. First, some teachers do not give a number for a beat that has no weight change. For example, the salsa may get called like this: "one two threeee, five six sevennnn," where the extended "threeee" and "sevennnn" account for the **hold–4** and **hold–8**, respectively. While that call works for folks who know the beat well, I think it's important for students struggling with the beat to hear a number or word called out on a beat with no weight change; otherwise it's easy to lose track of the beat.

## Dueling Counts: Musical Count and Pattern Count Juxtaposed

While the musical count is rarely heard in class, there is one common exception. As mentioned in Chapter 2, "Counting Music: Finding the Sets of 8," when teachers start a class dancing, they count you in by counting the last few beats of a set of 8, usually calling out something like ". . . and a five six seven eight." But when the dance starts, they switch to calling the pattern, which may be done with numbers or words. If they use numbers, I think it's important to recognize that they're now counting a step pattern and not the music. Music will be in sets of 8 throughout the song; pattern counts will usually be in groups of six or eight and can change with each new step pattern. This point is moot if you understand both counts. But to someone like me, when I was a struggling beginner, changing the rules of counting in the same breath really messed me up.

Second, *syncopations*, stepping between beats of music, add a little complexity.

Whoops, stop reading . . . at this point, things could get a little messy. If you have no intention of taking dance classes, and if you stick to just single and double rhythm, which is all you need to survive, feel free to skip the next several paragraphs on the **&** **count**. But if you're going to learn dances with syncopations, for example, any of the swing dances, you'll eventually need to grasp the **& count**. Plus, if you want to be a good dancer, getting a grip on the **& count** will help to improve your movement technique (Chapter 9, "Movement and Timing"). So this is a little advanced, but even total newbs should probably have a look.

Do you remember the triple rhythm, which steps between two beats of music on the **& count** (page 54)? Oh, the pain, the agony—the **& count**! That demure, innocent looking **&** was a concept that tormented me. I should call it the sneaky and diabolical **& count**, because it seemed like teachers pulled it out of thin air whenever they wanted. Sometimes they'd slip it in between numbers, sometimes they didn't; I didn't get it and it always threw me into a tailspin. Tailspins I didn't need.

Recalling that the beat marks time, the **&** identifies a point about halfway between two beats of music. Technically, every beat in a set of 8 has an **& count** like this:

## & COUNT

| MUSICAL COUNT | &1 | &2 | &3 | &4 | &5 | &6 | &7 | &8 |
|---|---|---|---|---|---|---|---|---|

But, when counting a step pattern, *the **& count** is vocalized only if there's a step or action on that particular **& count***. Contrast this to a beat of music; if there's no step on a beat, I encourage you to still vocalize it. For example, note the vocalizing of the **hold–4** and **hold–8** earlier for the salsa count. That's the essence of understanding the **& count**—it only gets vocalized if there's a weight change. A quick look at the triple rhythm and swing dancing will flesh it out some more.

The triple rhythm is counted like this: **1&2**, with weight changes on the **1**, the **&** and the **2**. Additionally, like singles and doubles, triple rhythm can start on any downbeat (**1**, **3**, **5** and **7**). So it can be danced in all of these locations: **1&2**, **3&4**, **5&6** and **7&8**.

The swing dances give beginners a lot of exposure to triple rhythm. East Coast swing and West Coast swing, different but related dances, use the same rhythm pattern, *double—triple—triple*. The pattern count for that rhythm pattern is **1 2—3&4—5&6**. Adding a verbal call and the rhythm pattern, it looks like this:

## SWING

| MUSICAL COUNT | 1 | 2 | 3 | | 4 | 5 | | 6 |
|---|---|---|---|---|---|---|---|---|
| PATTERN COUNT | 1 | 2 | 3 | & | 4 | 5 | & | 6 |
| VERBAL CALL | STEP | STEP | STEP-THREE-TIMES | | | STEP-THREE-TIMES | | |
| RHYTHM PATTERN | *double* | | *triple* | | | *triple* | | |

Remember, triples are *faster* than singles and doubles, which means the verbal call comes at you quicker and your feet have to move faster to stay on time. Any dance with triples is harder than a dance without triples. The Advanced Info Alert on page 67 gives the technique for dancing triple rhythm.

Once I learned the rule for counting the **& count**, it was easy to embrace and dance it. Other things fell into place too: verbal calls began to make more sense and my general timing improved, especially when to move my frame to keep my weight changes on time.

*Lingo Alert*: Musicians use the **& count** differently than dancers, so don't be confused if you hear the **& count** discussed in musical terms. The **& count** for dancers pertains to steps and other body movements, which are moot for musicians.

**ADVANCED INFO ALERT** There's another type of triple rhythm, but it's not something a beginner will encounter, with the exception of the cha-cha and the hustle. Skippy Blair calls it a *syncopated triple*. It can be danced in these locations: **&1 2**, **&3 4**, **&5 6** and **&7 8**. While it's still three steps in two beats of music, **&1 2** has a different look and feel than **1&2**. An advanced dancer could substitute a **&1 2** for a **1&2** to stylize a move—to make it look just a little different than the way others do the same move.

Let's put all this to use. Whenever I learn a new dance figure, I always identify the pattern count, as I learn a step quicker if the count is used to call the pattern. The count creates a logical and direct relationship between the step and the music, which makes it easier to remember and execute. If the teacher uses the count correctly, I'm all set. If a verbal call is used instead of the pattern count (that is, if words are used instead of numbers), or if an unfamiliar system of counting is used, I scramble to identify the correct pattern count. I use the five-step process on page 56 and just add a sixth step:

1. I listen for the downbeat and upbeat and sets of 8 to make sure I'm on the beat and connected to the music.

2. If the teacher doesn't announce it, I figure out how many beats are in the step pattern, which is usually six or eight (sometimes four).

3. I note which beats have weight changes, which beats have no weight changes and if there are any steps between beats of music. If I'm confused, this is when I ask the teacher questions, which are usually related to understanding the verbal call being used and when to make weight changes.

4. I identify the two-beat dance rhythms, which will be mostly single, double and triple rhythm.

5. I string the dance rhythms together to identify the rhythm pattern (for example, *double—single—double—single*) so the pattern will be easier to remember and to see how similar it is to other steps that I know.

## Advanced Info Alert: Intro to Waltz

| | | | | | | |
|---|---|---|---|---|---|---|
| **MUSICAL COUNT** | 1 | 2 | 3 | 4 | 5 | 6 |
| **PATTERN COUNT** | 1 | 2 | 3 | 4 | 5 | 6 |
| **VERBAL CALL** | FORWARD | SIDE | TOGETHER | BACK | SIDE | TOGETHER |
| **RHYTHM PATTERN** | | *waltz triple* | | | *waltz triple* | |

Waltz—both waltz the music and waltz the dance—is the exception to a number of rules. The waltz is beyond the scope of this book, but a quick look is important. Plus, if a woman ever drags you on the floor and you're pressed to do a waltz, you'll learn how to fake a waltz at the end of Chapter 13, "Survival Dancing." Many slow, romantic songs are waltzes, so knowing how to fake a waltz may score points.

Some teachers talk about waltz using *time signatures* (waltz has a 3/4 time signature, all other dance music is 4/4 or 2/4), but my brain shuts down when anyone talks time signatures. I don't want to compose music; I just want to entertain my partner for three minutes. For the casual dancer, I believe this is all you need to know: Waltz is counted in sets of 6, all other dance music is counted in sets of 8.

Sets of 6 can be heard because they're *in* the music.

A set of 6 has two three-beat dance rhythms and the **count 1** and **count 4** have an emphasis. A three-beat dance rhythm in waltz is structured *downbeat upbeat upbeat*. Three beats of waltz have a *down up up* feeling; and as you dance your head should go down, then up, then up again. This is referred to as the *rise and fall,* which define the look, feel and style of the dance.

Many people count waltz, both the music and the dance, **1 2 3—1 2 3**. Musicians count it that way too, because technically they create the music in three-beat measures. But for dancers it's best to count it **1 2 3—4 5 6**, which better reflects the natural pairing of measures and the true sentence structure of the melody or other themes in the music. Counting the basic step pattern in sets of 6 also follows the rule that a dance figure is not complete until the same foot is free again (see Advanced Info Alert page 77). A set of 6 is also called a mini-phrase, and the most common structure for a major phrase (page 36) is four sets of 6, which is 24 beats (4 × 6 = 24). For the man, a good verbal call is FORWARD SIDE TOGETHER—BACK SIDE TOGETHER, which would be a box step (a square-shaped step pattern) if you kept your orientation always looking forward (when dancing you don't—it's danced with a rotation).

**6.** I identify the pattern count by correlating the weight changes to the beat, which is easy to do once you know the rhythm pattern. I use the pattern count, calling it silently in my head, to learn and execute the step pattern.

The beauty of knowing how to count is that it tells you where you are in the pattern. Whether a teacher says, STEP STEP or WALK WALK or STEP TWICE or LEFT RIGHT or QUICK QUICK or **1 2** or **5 6** or BEE BOP or ROCK STEP or SIDE TOGETHER or FORWARD BACK, they all have one thing in common: two steps that are timed to occur as each word or number is spoken. But only **1 2** and **5 6** tell where you are in the rhythm pattern, which is what you need to know to break a pattern down, learn it and connect it to the music.

**TIP** Identifying the count is not easy at first but it's probably easier than it sounds. Of course, sometimes the easiest way to do it is just to yell out in class, "What's the count on this move?"

For a beginner, that's all there is to counting dance patterns. I entered dance-heaven when I finally learned the count. Rhythmic and musical structures didn't come naturally to me, so I needed the pattern count to lay a structural foundation in my brain—only then could I connect to the non-counting methods and begin to feel the music.

Guys, beware: When you're trying to learn a new pattern and are hopelessly lost, you may be surrounded, like I was, by great dancers who don't use the count. You'll hear them say, "I just feel it," or "I don't know how I do it—it's in the music, just listen."

## Counting Beats versus Counting Steps

I sometimes get hysterical over this because it kept me in a fog for years. The issue is, when counting a pattern, *what to count*. I believe it's best to count the beats of the step pattern, which connects you to the beat, and not the number of steps taken, which connects you to nothing and is an obstacle to learning the beat.

Here's the correct pattern count for salsa, which aligns it with the eight-beat structure of the music:

| MUSICAL COUNT | 1 | 2 | 3 | 4 | 5 | 6 | 7 | 8 |
|---|---|---|---|---|---|---|---|---|
| PATTERN COUNT | 1 | 2 | 3 | hold-4 | 5 | 6 | 7 | hold-8 |

But some may count salsa like this (note that by **count 5** in the music the pattern count is not aligned):

| MUSICAL COUNT | 1 | 2 | 3 | 4 | 5 | 6 | 7 | 8 |
|---|---|---|---|---|---|---|---|---|
| PATTERN COUNT | 1 | 2 | 3.... | | 4 | 5 | 6.... | |

or sometimes

| MUSICAL COUNT | 1 | 2 | 3 | 4 | 5 | 6 | 7 | 8 |
|---|---|---|---|---|---|---|---|---|
| PATTERN COUNT | 1 | 2 | 3.... | | 1 | 2 | 3.... | |

which counts the number of steps taken and completely ignores the eight-beat structure of the music (note that it would typically be pronounced, "one two threeee," where the extended "threeee" accounts for no steps on **hold-4** and **hold-8**).

If you really want to butcher the count for swing, **1 2—3&4—5&6**, I've heard it like this: **1 2—123—123**. Arghh . . . my head hurts. Maybe that count gets a bumbling beginner through a class, but that poor guy will never connect to the beat or the music and will never move past the beginner level.

Here's one for the record books. In my case, I had teachers

count the waltz and the polka the same. To my ear, they both were counted, "one two three, one two three." This led me to believe they were the same dance! For the unsuspecting newbie, I think counting the waltz and the polka the same will result in profound confusion. Fail, broken, abort, mayday. (The correct count for polka is **1&2—3&4**; and the correct count for the waltz is **1 2 3—4 5 6**.)

Sorry, I have to vent: I believe teachers who counted steps instead of beats stunted my progress. May a thousand space aliens do a conga line across your rooftops.

It'll make you feel inferior. Remember, they probably have talent; thankfully, we can count. If you get stuck, use the count.

**ADVANCED INFO ALERT** There are some eight-count patterns, like salsa and rumba, that are sometimes taught as four-count patterns. Don't sweat it; a four-count salsa pattern is just half of the eight-count pattern. So it's the same dance. Treating the salsa as an eight-count pattern makes it easier to naturally align or *phrase* to the sets of 8 in the music. The rule I go by is that *a pattern is not finished until the same foot is free again.* The merengue, *double—double,* and the samba, *triple—triple,* are examples of true four-count patterns, because the leader's left foot is free again on **count 4**. Also, although I've been treating all single rhythm and all double rhythm as eight-count patterns to help you connect to the sets of 8, you can look at them as four-count patterns too: *single—single* and *double—double,* respectively. It's easy to shorten or extend the length of patterns if you think of rhythms in terms of two-beat increments.

# PART 3

# Dancing

# Chapter 7

# Posture and Dance Frame

Those who dance are considered insane by
those who cannot hear the music.
— *Comedian George Carlin*

Posture and dance frame—finally something easy. Well, not really, but it's a nice change from all that rhythm and counting.

**Posture** is that thing you were bombarded with as a kid: stand up straight. It's important in dance not only because it makes you look good—part of looking good is creating nice lines with your body—but good posture makes you feel light in your partner's arms. While the posture for social dancing should be more relaxed than for competitive dancing, a poor posture will produce a sloppy-looking dance.

Good posture is easy: Do a self-exam in the mirror, realign a little and slouch no more! Okay, it won't be that easy, but mirrors don't lie and they're invaluable feedback. Other tools for checking posture are filming yourself with a video camera and asking your teacher to check.

Also, get to know what good posture feels like. Do this demonstration right now: Freeze for a moment, holding your body in its exact position. Notice that your shoulders may be shrugged or tense. Let them drop away from your ears. Physically and mentally shift all your upper body weight and tension to your lower body. Now, imagine being suspended from above; your head is erect, light and alert. Feel better?

**TIP** There's an added benefit to improving posture: Good posture will make you look young. Even better, it'll make you feel young. That's a basic principle of yoga: assume a vital posture and you revitalize your spirit.

**ANOTHER TIP** Body mechanics aside, the hardest part of improving posture is the thought process: improving posture requires attention of the mind to break bad habits.

## EXERCISE 10: POSTURE

Good posture for dancing goes a step further than just standing up straight. Hold your arms out to the side, horizontally, so they form a straight line with your shoulders—like a human **T**—palms facing down, thumbs facing forward. Then, rotate both hands 180 degrees so your thumbs go from pointing forward to pointing toward the back, palms facing up. As you rotate your hands let the muscles in your back pull down, as if they were making your hands rotate. You should feel a nice lift in the chest. As you pull down with the back muscles, they should have the feeling of locking into position. This is the feeling you want while dancing. I try to do a subtle version of this hand rotation and back lock (I do it with my hands at my side) as I walk on to the dance floor with my partner.

**Dance frame** is your stature, how you hold your arms in relation to your body, particularly the *tone* necessary for the arms and torso to create a solid but supple unit. Dance frame is important because when both partners have the proper frame, it allows the *connection* necessary for leading and following. When someone has poor tone in his or her arms it's sometimes referred to as spaghetti arms—they're limp, like wet noodles—and it's difficult to dance with someone like that. Tone is a feeling, so it's something you'll have to work on with a partner. There's more on connection in Chapter 10, "Lead and Follow." *Lingo Alert: Frame* can also be used anatomically to describe the upper part of the body, synonymous with the word *torso*, so the word *frame* needs to be taken in context. Again, the frame I'm describing here includes the muscle tone necessary to create a connection with your partner.

Dance frame is a little tricky as you want to have tone without being stiff. Your muscles are activated, and there's energy flowing through your arms and torso. But don't tighten your muscles; they should be a bit firm, yet soft. Most beginners are either too rigid or too limp. I find that beginning followers are usually too limp. Women who used to dance and think they still know how—what might be described as being rusty—are often stiff.

## EXERCISE 11: MAINTAIN DANCE FRAME

One of the challenging things for the beginner is to automatically maintain good posture and dance frame when you're preoccupied with everything else that makes a successful dance. Some muscle conditioning, some muscle memory, no problem. This is an isometric exercise (muscles held firm with no movement). Assume a good posture (see Exercise 10). Hold your arms out as if you were hugging a huge beach ball and raise them to chest level. It's best if you can simulate the frame of the standard, closed ballroom dance position discussed in Chapter 8, "Positions." Establish an energy level in your arms that's just enough to keep them extended without falling down; that's good tone. Check yourself in a mirror. Keep your attention solely on your posture and frame; constantly correct. Note the energy level in your arms—relaxed and not stiff. Try to hold this position—arms at chest level—for a few minutes. If you're super-new to dancing, you'll probably feel a little aching in your muscles quickly. Take a break, then repeat. Keep repeating but don't overdo it the first time or your muscles will be sore the next day. Repeat this exercise over several more days. The goal is for this—both the arm positioning and the tone—to become automatic and effortless; the key is to feel your back muscles lock into place. This is a good pose to hold when you mark rhythms and practice step patterns on your own. Even if your muscles feel achy in the beginning, they'll condition quickly.

They say that how you dance is a metaphor for who you are. How you carry yourself on the dance floor may be how you carry yourself through life. A droopy posture and dance frame could be interpreted (or misinterpreted) as a droopy person. True or false, the take away is this: don't slouch and think *tone.*

# Chapter 8

# Positions

We did an Argentine tango. She did some
fancy high kicks. It was very painful.

— *Rene Zgraggen, renez.com*

Finally, the time has come for you to touch your partner. Assume the position!

*Dance positions* are the different positions used for holding your partner. They tell you where you are in relation to your
partner and where to make contact. Perhaps you've seen couples
embracing as they foxtrot or waltz, or couples holding one hand as
they do swing or salsa, or couples spooning as they do a slow dance,
or couples all twisted into knots as they do country and western.

There's nothing mysterious about positions, although small
differences may exist between teachers. There are only a handful
of common positions and there is only one of great importance, the
*closed ballroom position,* which is the familiar-looking embrace
used in the basic step pattern of most social dances. For survival
dancing, the closed ballroom position will be your primary dance
position. *Freebie Video:* Check my website for links to visuals.

The stylistic details of the closed ballroom position, called
the **closed position** for short, can vary from dance to dance. For
example, the Latin dances are very erect. In contrast, East Coast
swing uses a closed position that's low to the floor (versus standing upright), with a lot of bend in the knees to create a rounded,
C-shaped dance frame. Also in East Coast swing, the bodies are
at a slight V-angle, as if partners were attached at one hip; and
the handhold is low and inverted.

Another position you may need is the *one-hand open position*, or just *open position* for short. It's not only common in the swing dances and salsa, but you'll use it for a handful of seconds anytime you do an underarm turn. From closed position, if you let go of her back with your right hand, you'll be in the one-hand open position. Simple as that. Essentially, you're just holding hands, your left to her right, and your bodies are separated. You both need good tone in your arms for the connection to work. Also, see page 95 on *partner centering*, which will help your connection in the open position.

Positions are relatively easy to pick up and are best learned on the dance floor, with a partner in hand, as you learn a new step pattern that requires a particular position. Dance classes do a good job of teaching positions. *Lingo Alert:* Depending upon the dance, the region of the country and the teacher, the same dance position can go by a variety of different names.

**TIP** It's common to incorrectly place your right hand on your partner's lower back in the closed position. Your hand should cup the base of her left shoulder blade. There's more on making contact with your right hand in Chapter 10, "Lead and Follow."

**ANOTHER TIP** I make use of simple variations to the closed position as an easy way to stylize a dance. For example, when I'm slow dancing in the closed position, I often lower my left hand, which is holding the follower's right hand, to waist level, to create a more relaxed and intimate look. Still holding her right hand, I may sometimes lay my left hand on my left hip, which I do for, maybe, eight beats of music, just to add style.

**YET ANOTHER TIP** If necessary, make adjustments to a dance position to accommodate each different partner. In other words, the mechanical details of a position may vary from partner to partner.

As you learn positions, keep in mind that to make a position look good you need good posture; and to make it work you need good dance frame. Also, check out the box on page 94, "Connection," for the dynamics of holding your partner.

# Chapter 9

# Movement and Timing

A degenerated and demoralizing musical system
is given a disgusting christening as "swing"
and turned loose to gnaw away the moral fiber
of young people.... Jam sessions, jitterbugs and
cannibalistic rhythmic orgies are wooing our
youth along the primrose path to Hell!

— *The Archbishop of Dubuque, 1938*

If you watch most beginners move on the dance floor they appear to be marching. I remember my marching days—they lasted almost a decade.

On the other hand, if you watch the masters move, they appear to effortlessly glide across the floor; they actually have the illusion of flight. That's the big question: How do you get from marching to flying? In Exercise 12 you'll learn the technique I use, but first some background.

There's a well-known rule of movement in dance: *foot follows frame*. The problem is that beginners do the opposite—they let their frame follow their foot—which gives the appearance of marching.

When I move, I find that it helps to think *frame* (torso) and not *step*. If you think *step* it creates a focus on the foot, which causes the foot to move first. Worse, the foot is often lifted too high and moved too far; the frame is then dragged sideways to catch the foot. This would be *frame follows foot*, the opposite of what you're trying to achieve. It looks clumsy and is a mark of a beginner. At worst, it looks like a game of hopscotch. Or a camel.

If you lead with your frame—if you move your torso first—the foot will naturally follow and, like a carpenter's plumb bob, reposition directly below your frame. Then, you simply lower your weight to finish the step. Unfortunately, this is much easier to utter than execute.

I've heard the concept of *foot follows frame* described, crudely, as leaning in the direction you want to move and then, just before you fall, the foot moves to catch your falling weight. Skippy Blair has a more precise and elegant technique. It'll be easiest to explain her method by jumping right into an exercise. First, three terms that Skippy uses (she coined *sending foot* and *receiving foot*):

> **center** the solar plexus, which is the point in the dance frame that's the focus of movement; *center* is short for *center point of balance. Lingo Alert:* Some teachers use the term *center* to identify the abdominal area, so you need clarification when that term is used.
>
> **sending foot** the weighted foot that presses into the floor to send the body
>
> **receiving foot** the unweighted foot that receives the weight change

## EXERCISE 12: TAKE A STEP

Do this first standing in place with small steps side-to-side. I mean really small steps, say, one to two inches, maybe three (see box "Take Baby Steps"). Once you can do a side step, then try a small walking step forward. Start with your weight on your right foot. Begin the step by pressing the sending foot, the weighted foot (the right foot), into the floor, which moves your body up and to the left. Imagine there is a tiny speed bump just to the left of your left foot. As your body rises and moves

## Take Baby Steps

Of all the things a beginner can do to improve and, especially, make life on the floor easier, this will give the greatest return for the least effort: *take baby steps*. Dance is not a contest for distance. You'll have enough trouble with what to move and when to move and which direction to move—don't make it harder by adding how far to move. Moreover, with a big step you tend to reach, which looks bad—frame will incorrectly follow the foot—and, with up-tempo music, you'll quickly exhaust yourself. What's important to your partner is not the distance covered but that there's a step—a weight change—and steps can be done in place. Oops, slight correction, what's really important is a weight change with good *timing* (more in a moment).

left, your receiving foot (left foot), which moves with your center, naturally and effortlessly crests the speed bump. When your center arrives at the new location, just one to two inches away—don't make me come over there to get you to take small steps—the receiving foot (left foot) will line up directly below. Then, just lower your weight onto your left foot. Next, still standing in place, try a step back to the other side (the right). When you're ready, try a small, walking step forward. At first do it slowly and exaggerate the motion, as if you were walking through chest-high water. Now here's the really hard part and the key to looking sharp: to time steps correctly when you do this to music, press and move your center on the **& count** (page 71), then lower your weight and hit the floor precisely on the beat (more on timing in a moment).

The key word for executing this movement technique is *press*, not *step*. It's a little counterintuitive, as the focus is not on the foot that takes the step but on the foot that's left behind, which does the work by pressing. Movement in any direction—

left, right, forward or back—can be accomplished with this technique of pressing into the floor. Think of a lion stalking prey. It will thrust its chest in the direction it wants to move and then the paws will follow. Think lion.

**ADVANCED INFO ALERT** There's a common body movement in dance called *contra body movement*. It's simply an exaggeration of the movement your body naturally makes when you walk: as the left foot goes forward, the left shoulder goes back and the right hip goes forward, all in one motion; as the right foot goes forward, right shoulder goes back and left hip goes forward, all in one motion. However subtle, this is how we walk naturally, especially when we're confident; this is how you should move when you mean business, whether it's into a job interview or on the dance floor. It's a bit of a strut, like how a matador walks. Where's my cape?

## EXERCISE 13: WALK WITH CONTRA BODY

As you walk, see if you can identify your natural contra body motion (see the previous Advanced Info Alert). Exaggerate the motion, making sure you're thrusting your center (solar plexus) ahead of your feet by pressing into the floor with the sending foot. Check yourself in a mirror. Pretend you're a matador.

How you move is pretty darn important, as it not only corrects that dorky look but also affects your ability to lead. If your center moves first, it feels good to your partner; and lead and follow will be much easier. A follower can feel a weight change coming, because she feels it first in your upper body, which moves before you step. If your feet move first it feels bad to your partner, and lead and follow will be awkward at best. But movement, any movement, will not look good or feel good to your partner without good timing.

**Timing** is controlling the speed of body movement in relation to the music. Specifically, this means getting the foot, the frame and the weight change to come together, simultaneously, exactly on the beat. Yes, your frame—your solar plexus—needs to be on time too. If you're early or late, even just a teeny-tiny bit, it's *off time*. Simple? Yes. Easy? Not!

Think of a pianist. For a chord to be played on the beat, the pianist can't move his hand and hit the chord at the same time. But by moving the hand into position before the beat, to a point right above the piano keys, hitting the chord on the beat is easy by simply lowering the hand. Likewise, if the dancer moves his center into position before the beat—on the **& count** (page 71), the point between two beats of music—then it's easy to hit the floor precisely on the beat by simply lowering his center.

Movement and timing are a couple of the hardest elements in dance to master. You can practice them as you mark rhythms and go over step patterns on your own. I still struggle with them. For us mortal, ungifted dancers, I've come to accept that doing this stuff perfectly takes at least two lifetimes.

*Lingo Alert:* I hate to be so picky about language but, hey, my mission is to make sense of the stuff that makes no sense. Some people use the word *timing* to identify the pattern count; for example when counting a double rhythm, two steps taken to two beats of music, someone might say the timing is "**1 2**." Also, the word *timing* is sometimes used to label the speed or tempo of the music; for example, someone might say the timing of the music is fast (call me obstinate, call me annoying, but tempo is a far more accurate label). You know the drill: take the word *timing* in context and ask questions if you get lost.

# Chapter 10

# Lead and Follow

Dancing is just a conversation between two
people . . . talk to me.

— *Harry Connick, Jr., to Sandra Bullock in* Hope Floats

**NOTE** *This entire chapter deserves an Advanced Info Alert.
Unlike music and rhythm, which you can work on by yourself,
lead and follow is something to do with a partner. Even then,
first time on the floor, it's tough to learn to lead and it should not
be your immediate focus; learn a step pattern first. Also, it's best
done in the context of a particular dance, which, for this book, is
survival dancing—doing simple footwork in the closed ballroom
position. One more thing: Traditionally, men lead and women
follow, a preference that persists today. Sorry if I offend anyone,
but this book is written for men who want to lead.*

"Catch many fish with those earrings?"

Guys, have you ever conversed with a woman using a line
like that? I haven't, but I've stumbled through countless dances
"conversing" like that. If only I'd known how to lead. Dance is
a conversation between two people, and lead and follow is the
language. Before I knew how to lead, my dancing annoyed many
partners.

It was odd. I would be on the beat and knew the pattern.
Yet, too often, things went horribly wrong. I'd lead this way, she'd
go that way. I'd lead an inside turn, she'd make an outside turn.
I'd move, she wouldn't. And thump. We'd bump.

Part of my confusion was the illusion that I knew how to
lead, which came from the assumption that I could learn to lead
in class. While classes are a start, it's hard to learn from classes

alone. The real progress will come from practicing patterns on the social dance floor—trial and error—with a variety of followers. In particular, work with partners who don't know your patterns and, every once in a while, with partners better than you (dancing up). Check out the box titled, "Three Reasons Why It's Hard to Learn to Lead in Most Dance Classes." While you can't learn to lead from a book either, I'll wander through some things that'll make the road from klutz to Casanova a little easier.

Let's start with definitions (from the Golden State Dance Teachers Association): A **lead** is an indication of direction. **Following** is a reaction to a lead. How do you *indicate*? That depends on the dance and the step pattern. At more advanced levels of dancing, you often want your partner to do something different; but to do a basic survival dance—to shuffle around in closed position—you want her to do what you do. When you move left, she moves left; in other words, you move together. To indicate, when you are survival dancing, just hold her gently without pushing, pulling or hunching over her. Hold her like you are holding a woman, in other words.

This may come as a shock to the cavemen I hear women complain about, but the leader does not use arm muscles to move his partner around the floor. That results in the dreaded *arm lead*. I know; the temptation is there because we're strong and we've got her in our hands. But an indication is more subtle and complex. It's a minimalist expression—no pushing, no pulling, no force—that's the skill behind leading. Interpreting the indication is the skill of following. Guys, muscling and dragging a follower around the floor is not leading. It's annoying.

Imagine you were holding a pillow in the closed position. The pillow is wedged between your right hand and your chest. If you want the pillow to go left, you step to the left and you and the pillow move left together. It's as simple as that. If you were to push the pillow to the left (while standing still), it would separate from your chest and fall.

When you're in the closed position, your most important point of contact is your right hand, which is cupping the base

## Connection

The concept of a dance *connection* is a biggie—and a hard one to put into words. For all I know, connection is some sort of mystical, magical force field, which links and unites you to your partner, because with a great follower, that's what it feels like. For the beginner, just think of it in the obvious sense of the word: the link or association you have with your partner. I'll try to describe it a little bit.

One of the most important elements for achieving a good connection is having tone in your muscles. Tone, first discussed on page 82, is that energy level in your muscles that's . . . how to put it . . . let's say, a little firm but supple. When you first embrace in the closed position, you will immediately be aware of the tone in her body—and she will feel the tone in yours. Your left hand should feel some resistance, which is what you want. Otherwise she will feel too stiff, like an immovable wall, or too loose, like a wet noodle. She wants to feel a little resistance too, not a brick wall or a spaghetti arm.

You both want to feel something at the point of contact of your right hand on her back. When she feels the tone of your hand on her back, she matches it by leaning back—by pressing her back into your hand. As she pushes back a little, you sort of pull in a little. This gives you a feeling of resistance—a push–pull–springy kind of feeling—and it gives you "something to work with." None of this will happen if you're a beginner and she's a beginner, but you can be conscious of it and begin to discover how good tone creates a connection.

The goal of a survival dancer is the ability to dance with any kind of partner. You will have to dance with those who lean in and those who lean out and those who just stand there and do nothing. Be prepared for everything. I've had followers who move in like I'm flypaper and she's a fly; and I've had followers who lean back hard like they were trying to escape. I've had them with blouses so slippery that my right hand couldn't maintain contact; and I've had them with so much hair it was hard to find their shoulder blade. Speaking of hair, I once had a partner with a long, thick ponytail, and every time she turned she whacked me in the face with it. The point of my little tangent is that every partnership is different, so expect the unexpected and take it in stride.

TIP Generally, you have better control moving side-to-side than moving forward and back. If she leans in, which won't give you the best connection, you'll probably have more success dancing in place with a side-to-side motion. On page 103 I discuss the basic side step, which should be relatively easy to lead with anyone.

ANOTHER TIP If you feel nothing in your right hand, pull her in a little closer.

TIP FOR FOLLOWERS If you feel nothing on your back, lean out by pressing back and into his hand on your back.

of her left shoulder blade. Note that your right hand is directly in front of you even though you can't see it. Imagine there's a rod going from the palm of your right hand, through the base of her left shoulder blade and into your solar plexus. As you dance in closed position—forward, back, side, rotate, whatever—think about always keeping your right hand directly in front of you. Now, without having to think about moving her, she will go wherever you go. So, in essence, just focus on doing your dance frame correctly and not on how you're going to keep her in front of you or how you're going to make her go left or right or forward or back. The positioning of your dance frame will *indicate* where you'd like her to go.

TIP In the closed position, avoid using the fingertips of your right hand, which are on the base of her left shoulder blade. Make full contact with your hand, especially the soft, cuplike part of your hand. Imagine you were holding a baby in that one hand (in terms of contact, not positioning). Also, make sure you cradle underneath her shoulder blade; it should feel a bit like she's sinking down into your hand. With your hand higher up it restricts her movement and may cause her to lose her balance.

*Partner centering* is another way that you can use your body positioning to indicate. Most of the time it's the job of your

## Three Reasons Why It's Hard to Learn to Lead in Most Dance Classes

**1.** *Lead and follow are not stressed in most classes.* Occasionally you'll find a class that spends time on lead and follow, maybe even a dedicated lead and follow class, but the vast majority of all classes are focused on teaching just step patterns, the more the better. Hopefully, you'll get some lead and follow tips, but not always. If you do get pointers, they're not usually stressed; and if you're more interested in flirting with your partner, you'll miss them.

**TIP** "What's the lead on that move?" If you're a teacher and I'm in your class, that's the question I'll be tossing your way broken-record-style. Get in the habit of asking that question when the lead and follow are not clear. Sometimes I'm more specific: "What's the timing on that lead?" These are good questions to ask a teacher after class too. For me, it was always a prelude to the teacher demonstrating the move with me, an easy way to dance up.

**ANOTHER TIP** When I dance up with better dancers, someone who I know and who will be honest, I sometimes ask for feedback: "How was the lead on that move?"

**2.** *Your partner always knows what's coming.* This is the real culprit. If lead and follow is a conversation, a dance class is like reading from a script. The teacher tells you what to lead, which your partner is privy to, so there's no spontaneity, no surprise. The follower knows both the move and when it's coming, so she can compensate for a bad lead. That's not how things will go down on the social dance floor with a follower who didn't take that class.

**3.** *In a beginners' class, you and you partner are just beginners.* By definition, you and your partner are not dancers yet. Take tennis: In a beginning tennis class, volleys are short in duration and balls hit the net more often, but play with an advanced student and volleys last longer. I made little progress with leading until I started, every once in a while, dancing up. For me, it was one of the best ways to get an accurate feel for lead and follow, to learn what works and what doesn't work.

**TIP** Don't dismiss partners who can't dance—they may be the bulk of your partners (plus, they're easy to impress, if that's your game). A good test of your skill as a leader is the ability to successfully lead a move with someone who is not an experienced follower. I have one fun move—rolling off each other's backs—which seems complicated but I can lead it with a non-dancer. It always get a big smile from my partner, like she's thinking, *yeah, he's the man!*

follower to stay centered on you, which creates a connection from your solar plexus to her solar plexus. Even when there's no contact, the feeling is like you're physically connected by some sort of . . . ah, this is a tough one . . . some sort of magnet or some sort of imaginary, bungee-cord-like hydraulic arm. Whoa, bad imagery—better to jump right into an exercise, which uses the "flashlight technique" (from the Golden State Dance Teachers Association). For now, just visualize yourself doing this with a partner. Note that the concept of centering is not as critical when you're in the closed ballroom position, but it will come into play when you're in the one-hand open position.

## EXERCISE 14: CENTER ON YOUR PARTNER

This exercise is probably more for followers, and it's a good one to do with a practice partner. Square off in front of her with your shoulders parallel, as if you were mirror images, about a foot or so apart. Keep this distance constant, and no touching. Now, as you move around the floor—backward, forward, left, right and rotating—your follower centers on you. Both you and your partner imagine you have a flashlight in your solar plexus. She keeps the light focused on your solar plexus and you aim your light at either your follower or in the direction you want her to travel. This creates a strong connection without the need for arm leading. Start slowly to let your follower get in the groove. Followers, try not to let the beam of light break away from his solar plexus; if it does, just gracefully return to it. Feel the connection, which is kind of like a magnet. Ladies, point your flashlight at his chin and you'll get a little lift that will improve your posture. Guys, I know, it seems a little counterintuitive because we normally use our arms to move objects from one place to another, not our chest. But it's a wonderful thing when you figure it out: leading with your solar plexus uses no force; and if your partner knows how to center, you can achieve an almost magical control over her. Learn this well.

**TIP** After you learn some step patterns and you give a lead and it fails—either you give a bad lead or she misinterprets it—resist the temptation to correct it with muscle power, which will result in a dreaded arm lead. If I attempt a lead and it fails, I lighten my lead, smile and go with her flow. If I don't get a dirty look, I'll come back to that move and try it again. I assume it was my fault and I figure out a way to do my part better. I keep experimenting and practicing the move until it works.

**TIP FOR FOLLOWERS** If you get a bad lead or a lead that's unclear, smile and do what you think he led. Part of your job is to make him look good, a basic rule of a good dance partnership.

## EXERCISE 15: SWITCH ROLES

Leaders should try following and followers should try leading. This is a great exercise, and learning the opposing part could dramatically improve your dancing. If you try following and feel the difference between a good lead and a bad lead, you can improve your leading. If your follower tries leading, she can improve her following. 'Nuff said.

Connecting with someone on the dance floor isn't always logical. You'll probably have the most fun dancing with women at your own level, and you're probably going to dance the most with followers who follow you best. That doesn't mean they're the best followers. While there are rules for lead and follow, they are tempered by a subjective side: chemistry. Like conversation, for whatever reasons, you will connect with some on the dance floor and not with others. People are compatible in dance like they are compatible in conversation. If you converse well and dance well with someone, make note: you may have a connection that goes beyond dance.

# Chapter 11

# Step Patterns

No move is too tricky, no spin too excessive.
For my partner.

*— John Hayes, whoever the heck he is*

The primary focus of most dance classes is step patterns. You're fed patterns and then more patterns. You'd think Moses had patterns on those tablets.

While step patterns are important—it's mostly through step patterns and styling that one dance is distinguished from another—I've always had an edgy relationship with them. You see, I'm certain I've forgotten at least 99.9 percent of the patterns that I've been taught. Patterns, shmatterns.

Yet I still love to learn a new step pattern.

**Step patterns** combine direction of movement, which includes foot positions, with a rhythm pattern. Step patterns essentially define the bigger motion a couple makes moving around the floor. Other labels you'll hear include *step*, *figure*, *move* and just *pattern* for short. (*Lingo Alert:* The word *pattern* has different meanings so it should always be taken in context.) *Move* is a fun word, a bit of slang, something to use in casual conversation—as in "check out that move"—although it can also be used to label any action, such as a styling move or a syncopation with your feet.

Learning simple step patterns at the beginner level should be easy, but a pattern is the point where everything comes together—movement, timing, rhythm, lead—so it can get hairy at times, especially if you have trouble hearing the beat. Even though I forget patterns quickly, I'm pretty good at learning new ones. Still, I've sucked in some nasty hairballs over the years.

When learning a new step pattern, I make quick mental notes on the following:

1. How many beats of music (usually six or eight)?
2. What's the rhythm pattern?
3. What's the pattern count?
4. What's a good verbal call?
5. Do I step forward, back, left, right or rotate?
6. What are the foot positions (feet together, feet shoulder width apart, and so on)?
7. Where does my left hand go? My right hand? Are there any hand changes?
8. Is my body parallel or angled to my partner?
9. If there are turns, do I turn left or right? Do I turn my partner left or right?
10. Is there anything special about the lead?

Every dance has a *basic pattern*, also called the *basic*, the primary pattern that distinguishes the dance. The basic pattern is usually, but not always, the easiest pattern and the first one taught. Each dance also has many additional patterns that fit the dance, and these may or may not have the same number of beats as the basic. In fact, patterns can be any number of even beats, although most patterns are six or eight beats long, sometimes four. That took me a while to understand, and my ignorance is now so obvious: If you can't find the beat nor count the music, the number of beats in a pattern is meaningless.

**ADVANCED INFO ALERT** Patterns can be *extended*. For example, you can turn a six-count step pattern with one turn into an eight-count pattern by adding a second turn. That's the kind of stuff you need to be able to do at the intermediate level.

Some good news. Just as different dances can share the same rhythm pattern, different dances can share the same step patterns. The *box step*, an easy and popular step that gets its name because the footwork creates a square, is not only the basic step for both rumba and waltz; it's also often used in foxtrot. Most patterns in salsa also work in mambo and cha-cha. Perhaps the most popular of all patterns, a basic *underarm turn*—leader lifts his arm, follower goes under it—is found in some form in most dances.

TIP An underarm turn (UAT) is an easy step pattern to slip into most dances, especially a survival dance. It's intuitive: you raise your left arm, she walks under it. Even when it's done poorly, it still looks like an underarm turn. Even if you and your partner have very little dance experience, if you raise your left arm, it's a good bet she'll try to go under it. She may rush it, she may be late, she may turn the wrong way and discombobulate the entire move, but most of the time followers attempt and succeed in going under your arm. If you lose the beat during the turn, no problem, just pick it up immediately after the UAT. For a variation, you can do the turn: just raise your left arm and you walk under your arm (sometimes differentiated as "his" UAT, versus "her" UAT).

I'm always on the hunt for versatile moves that can be used in more than one dance. I also look for patterns that are easy to remember and, especially, easy to lead with a new partner. Followers tell me all the time that they like simple choreography as it gives them time to work on their dance skills, like styling and syncopations (footwork). To a follower, a dance packed with complicated, fancy moves, especially if the guy doesn't lead them well, is not fun. It's exhausting.

Over the years, I always wondered about the difference between a good partner and a great partner. Great partners were effortless, as if they gave me energy and I could dance for days. On the other hand, some "good" partners made me run my butt off. I think part of the answer lies in the notion that a dancer should execute a step pattern a little differently with each part-ner. This tweaking has to accommodate the uniqueness of each partner; that is, every partner dances differently and you should dance a little differently with every partner. But don't try too hard to adjust. Just let it happen naturally. If you don't adjust,

## The Side Step

| MUSICAL COUNT | 1 | 2 | 3 | 4 | 5 | 6 | 7 | 8 |
|---|---|---|---|---|---|---|---|---|
| PATTERN COUNT | 1 | 2 | 3 | hold-4 | 5 | 6 | 7 | hold-8 |
| VERBAL CALL | SIDE | TOGETHER | SIDE | TOUCH | SIDE | TOGETHER | SIDE | TOUCH |
| RHYTHM PATTERN | double | | | single | double | | | single |

For survival dancing, a good pattern to know is the *side step*. It's as easy as they come, and it's versatile. It's sort of a shuffle to the left and then a shuffle to the right, using the closed position (Chapter 8, "Positions"). It uses the same rhythm pattern as salsa (page 69), *double—single—double—single*. A good verbal call for this eight-count step pattern is SIDE TOGETHER—SIDE TOUCH—SIDE TOGETHER—SIDE TOUCH.

*Freebie Video:* Look for a video clip on my website that demonstrates the leader's footwork—the *floor pattern*—for the side step.

The following is a description of the floor pattern. Start with your feet together, weight on the right. Take tiny steps, just a few inches—remember, it's never about distance:

On **count 1**: Step left (SIDE). Weight is on your left.

On **count 2**: Step your right foot together (TOGETHER) and do a weight change. Your feet are now together, weight on the right.

On **count 3**: Step left again (SIDE). Weight is back on your left.

On **count 4**: Bring your right foot together and touch your right toe (TOUCH) to the floor with no weight change. Your weight is still on your left. Get ready to reverse direction and repeat this shuffle to the right.

On **count 5**: Step right (SIDE). Weight is on the right.

On **count 6**: Then step your left foot together (TOGETHER). Weight is on the left.

On **count 7**: Step right again (SIDE). Weight is on the right.

On **count 8**: Bring your left foot together and touch your left toe (TOUCH) to the floor but no weight change. The weight is still on your right and you are back where you started.

## To Travel or Not To Travel

While we're on the subject of moving around the floor, when doing a survival dance you will probably dance in place, in one spot, which is easier than traveling around the floor. If people are traveling and bumping into you, avoid them by moving toward the center of the floor.

**ADVANCED INFO ALERT**

Be conscious of the flow of traffic on the floor. *Progressive* dances, the dances that move around the floor (foxtrot, waltz, tango, country two-step), move counterclockwise around the perimeter, which is called the *line of dance* (LOD). Faster couples should stick to the outside and slower-moving couples should move toward the center a bit. (I'm not a trained country and western two-stepper; so if I hug the outer perimeter on a floor of experienced dancers, I get trampled. To fake my two-step, I've learned to find that zone between the perimeter and the center where couples travel at my speed.) A *spot* dance is a dance that stays in one spot (the Latin and swing dances). If you want to do a spot step pattern while doing a traveling dance, break away from the LOD and move toward the center. A dance floor can be mixed; for example, you can do East Coast swing (spot) and foxtrot (progressive) to a lot of the same music.

your dancing will seem overbearing or disconnected and, to make the dance work, your partner is forced to do extra work. Ideally, both sides should contribute to making it work, and both sides should make whatever adjustments they feel need to be made. This won't always happen, but it's best to still do your part.

The creation or choice of a step pattern and how you string patterns together is called *choreography*. A string of step patterns is often called an *amalgamation* or a *routine*. Choreography is our job, guys, and it can be a challenge: I don't know how many times I've gone out for a night of dancing with, say, six patterns remembered from class, only to promptly forget five of the six the moment I step on the floor. Even after you remember patterns, there's a skill to matching patterns with the music, as well as a skill in choosing one pattern that will flow into the next. Group classes are a good way to learn new patterns, and good teachers will choreograph their routines to flow and to match the music.

Speaking of choreography, I make a distinction between two types. First, there's planned choreography, which is what you would see at a performance or a competition. For the beginner, I also consider choreography to be planned when, dancing socially, you take all the patterns you remember from class and string them together in a long, encyclopedic routine without any regard to the music or your partner. You repeat the same routine for every dance.

Then there's *spontaneous social dancing*, which is the choreography you do automatically, without thinking. It's something you'll see only at a social dance (one exception: *Jack and Jill* competitions where your partner and the music are unknown in advance). Spontaneous social dancing is unplanned; you put stuff together as you go along, on the fly, as you respond to what's happening in the music and with your partner.

For me, performances and competitions are not as interesting to watch as spontaneous social dancing. Planned choreography lacks freshness and the element of surprise. Also, performances and competitions often lack a real dance connection

---

### My Pet Peeve: Step Pattern Mania

Many dancers equate how good a dancer they are to how many step patterns they know. Not! Remember, the best followers say you can be a great leader with just five or six patterns. Of course, that's six perfectly led patterns, on the beat, with good timing, connected to the music and to her. But that's my point: Don't focus on the quantity of patterns to the detriment of perfecting a few. Please, look beyond the step patterns and try to see that a well-executed, simple pattern pleases the eye—and your partner—more than a poorly executed cool pattern.

because the follower always knows what's coming; choreography that's planned does not require true lead and follow. On the other hand, spontaneous social dancing is raw and instinctive, and it requires a real connection. Eventually, you improvise; you make up stuff and make the dance your own—that's the goal of a great social dancer. Take the highest ranking competitive dance couple in the world and I'd much rather watch them dance socially than during a competition—say, at midnight, surrounded by other couples so they think nobody's watching and they take risks and try new moves. That's dancing on the edge.

## EXERCISE 16: STYLE THE FREE HAND

I know what you're thinking, styling is not part of step patterns, but I didn't know where to put this. I think you'll thank me in a moment as this exercise is easy and it'll help to take the edge off of looking like a beginner. Let's look at a specific styling choice, the free hand, which is a hand (or hands) not connected to your partner. It's a hand that floats free. For example, if you were in the one-hand open position (page 86), your right hand would be free. You can also have a free hand during a step pattern. For example, if you were executing an underarm turn, for the several beats it takes to turn your partner, your right hand would be free (your left hand is turning her). I pick on the free hand as it's easy to see, it's easy to adjust, it contributes a lot to making nice body lines and it can add both personal and dance style to a move. Also, I pick on the free hand because a free hand that's lifeless and dead screams "beginner" at me. Watch the dance floor for free hands. What do most people do with their free hands? Do they extend their hands to create nice lines? Do their hands exude energy? Do their hands contribute to the dance style? Look at the detail: Is the palm up or down and are the fingers open or closed? Watch an old

## Styling

*Styling* adds coolness to your dance. I'm always on the lookout to steal a good styling move.

**Styling** is the thing you add that gives the look, feel and essence to a dance. Styling generally refers to the *dance style,* something common to that dance that all dancers do. But there's also *personal style,* the creative influence only you do that changes the look and feel of a dance.

Styling, both dance and personal, spans a broad range: footwork, hand positioning, posture and dance frame, body lines, body isolations, body shaping, patterns, syncopations, improvisation, the energy exuded, eye contact, facial expression, a rock or a sway or a bounce, grace or charm, and sex appeal. It could be anything that makes the dance look different—or like you own it. You can pick up dance styling tips in classes that focus on step patterns, but occasionally it's possible to find dedicated styling classes for more popular dances. Of course, you can also learn styling by watching other dancers. Where's that Fred Astaire DVD?

Fred Astaire movie—what does he do with his free hand? As you dance, be conscious of what you do with your free hand. If it's "dead"—if it's hanging down by your side, lifeless—try keeping it at or a little above your waist as if it were floating on top of waist-deep water (elbows bent and relaxed). This is the default position for your hand (or hands), and it's where it (they) should be if not doing anything else. Give your free hand energy and attitude. *Advanced Exercise:* Watch the dance floor, pick someone you like and mimic something cool they do with their free hand.

# PART 4

# Survival

# Chapter 12

# *Slow Dancing*

Never give a sword to a man who can't dance.

*— Often attributed to Confucius*

You're at a bar or a nightclub or a wedding or a New Year's Eve party. A slow song is played, and within seconds the floor is flooded with couples embracing and swaying. Standing alone and looking left out, you grow tense. With the heat rising around your collar, you eye a woman in the distance and make your move. You approach and, with a choked voice, utter one word: "Dance?" Unexpectedly, she accepts. If you were Travolta or Swayze or Secret Agent 007, you'd sweep her off her feet. What will you do?

When I was a beginner I found myself in that predicament many times. What kind of dance should I do? Is it okay to make body contact with a stranger? How close should I get? Does she think I'm flirting? Have I made too much contact? Have I made too little contact? Is she having a good time?

I'll return to body contact in a moment. First, let's look at the dance. I'll finish this chapter by looking at some options for lessons, because it may be hard to find classes labeled "slow dancing."

Slow dancing is a curious phenomenon. It's not taught much at dance studios; you don't get any good hits when you search online for it; it's not easily defined; nor is there a widely accepted curriculum. Yet it may be the one dance that every guy wishes he could do. And while it's not easily defined, most people, including non-dancers, probably know it when they see it. How can slow dancing be both mainstream and enigmatic?

Slow dancing can take many forms, and it changes over time. But most **slow dancing** has its roots in the foxtrot, and it's just the mixing of single and double rhythm to slow music. The foxtrot is a smooth, elegant and versatile dance that fits easily to slow and romantic music. Much of the dancing that Fred Astaire and Ginger Rogers performed in their movies during the 1940s and 1950s was a foxtrot, and I have watched their movies to steal moves for my slow dancing.

Whatever you call it, the key to slow dancing is to get comfortable mixing single and double rhythm, which is exactly what survival dancing is all about (Chapter 13, "Survival Dancing"). Basic slow dancing is just survival dancing to slow music, plus some sensual styling like body contact. The next chapter will introduce you to some different ways to use single and double rhythm, including the simplest of all dances, a *sway*, which is one way to get through a slow dance if you don't know what you're doing.

The one aspect of slow dancing that can't wait until the next chapter is the body contact, the getting in close, the sensual embrace. For many, it may be why you want to learn dance. While body contact isn't necessary for a slow dance—see box "How to Slow Dance with Your Mother-in-Law"—it's fun and adds an unequivocal element of intimacy.

Some degree of body contact in partner dancing is not uncommon. In any dance that uses the closed position, body contact often happens naturally and effortlessly, especially if you have a good connection with a familiar or experienced partner. Certain dance positions and certain moves, like a dip, will put you in closer contact with your partner. In two dances, Argentine tango and Balboa, contact is standard technique. While contact can occur anywhere from thighs to heads depending upon the dance, the move, the styling and the physical size of your partner, when making contact in the closed position to improve the dance connection, contact is in the upper body, diaphragm-to-diaphragm. This is the area where you should "let it happen."

For the reluctant dancer, making contact can be intimidating—too intimate, too awkward and too not-good-enough-to-pull-it-off. To my chagrin, I discovered that to do a graceful dance while stuck together requires some skill—from both partners. Before I could consistently keep the beat and give a decent lead, I had many awkward, forgettable slow dances. If both dancers don't step on the beat together when connected, well, think bumper cars at an amusement park.

I like to start a slow dance with an unfamiliar partner with some inches of separation, and I'll keep this separation for as long as it takes to establish a true dance connection. In particular, I'll be conscious of her frame since, to do it well, to make contact not seem aggressive, you need her help by way of a relaxed or inviting frame. I find that if my partner is also entertaining the notion of a close embrace, our receptive frames will, mysteriously, close the gap. I sometimes test the water by ever-so-gently guiding her closer, but if there's reluctance in her frame, any stiffness at all, I abort immediately. I check her face at this point: Any hint of discomfort and I know to keep some distance. My experience is that there will be many ambiguous situations where you won't quite know what's happening (ahem, just like in real-life relationships).

TIP FOR FOLLOWERS If you want to resist a leader, let your left thumb strategically slip down to the front part of his right shoulder, which will allow you to apply outward pressure or, literally, push him away. Also, the crotch is not a legitimate point of contact for leading, so do not accept a "crotch lead" from a leader if it offends you.

## How to Slow Dance with Your Mother-in-Law

Making body contact is not inherently sleazy nor necessarily sexual. It's not unusual for two good dancers, dancing any style of any dance, to have some contact when in the closed position. But when a slow song is played, which will coax many couples into a close embrace, it's not necessary, nor at times desirable—say, when dancing with your mother-in-law—to make contact to have a satisfying slow dance.

Depending upon the situation, I may close the normal gap of four to five inches, used in the closed position, to one or two inches to suggest more intimacy. I may close the gap so our clothes touch; at that point, there's no daylight between us so the visual effect is body contact. Or I might make very light and minimal contact. In lieu of contact I might stylize the dance to suggest more intimacy, such as adding a few dips (if she's not an experienced dancer I do it carefully—see page 117). If I want to avoid intimacy, I'll do patterns that open us up, such as underarm turns. Fear not, if you're called into service to slow dance with a partner you don't want to get close to, you can do it and make it fit on a floor of slow dancing.

I believe there's a benefit to starting a dance with some separation and establishing a connection to show her you know how to dance. By gaining her confidence before making contact, I believe you will get better results than rushing in with the immediate-contact method, which may get you rebuffed for the full three minutes. Besides, people often need deniability—*well we started innocently and he was a good dancer and everything so we had this connection and one thing led to another.* . . . Ultimately, whether to make contact is her choice, and etiquette dictates that we respect her wishes. Always be prepared to abort.

There's an old saying that dance is a vertical expression of a horizontal thought. While I'll leave further body contact, below the waist, up to your imagination, I do believe that full body contact, to improve the art, can be done, if not innocently, at least constructively. After all, if both partners are into it and if more contact makes the connection better, then the partnership can be strengthened and the dancing can move to a higher level. Of course, at this point, art may not be the only objective—but that's why we're all here anyway, right?

TIP Empty your front pockets, especially the front right pocket. You'll mostly do a slow dance in some form of the closed position. Your body will be slightly offset to the left so that your right foot is positioned between her two feet. As you move in it will be your right side that makes contact first. I find stuff in my pockets distracting. So, ritualistically, I empty them before I enter a dance. Or at least I move stuff from the right side to the left or front to back. For a serious night of dancing, I James-Bondishly put my keys, cash and credit cards in an ankle wallet.

While it's possible to find dedicated classes in slow dancing, this may prove surprisingly difficult. They might go under a slightly different name, like "nightclub slow dance" or "nightclub foxtrot"; so it's always worth calling a studio and asking. Here are a couple of other options:

- Slow dancing draws so much from foxtrot that it's usually a good place to start, although the connection to slow dancing may not seem obvious right away. Perhaps request from the teacher a demonstration of how to apply the foxtrot to slow dancing and ask for tips on how to stylize the foxtrot to create a slow dance. Also, a foxtrot class will probably teach a six-count basic pattern (*double—single—single* or *single—single—double*), and it's best to think of the slow dancing basic as an eight-count pattern (*double—single—double—single*) so it's easier to stay phrased (aligned) to the sets of 8 in the music.

- I think rumba is another dance that would help in learning to slow dance, as it's an easy dance, it's romantic, it uses slower tempos and the rumba basic uses the preferred rhythm pattern, *double—single—double—single.*

- Perhaps the most interesting choice today to learn slow dancing would be classes in "blues dancing," which is what the Lindy Hop community calls a type of slow dancing that has roots in the swing era of the 1930s. Blues dancing draws from dances like the *grind* and the *slow drag* (both have lots of body contact) and something done at the Savoy Ballroom in Harlem in the 1930s called *ballrooming,* which was a slow, slinky and somewhat satirical rendition of the foxtrot. Blues dancing is undergoing a revival, and classes and weekend workshops are available. While the music is classic slow-dancing music—jazz and blues, with slower tempos, from around the 1930s—there's no set dance curriculum; so you'll see a wide variety of teaching. Also, with medium-tempo songs, it can look more like swing than slow dancing because so many people come from the swing movement, which uses a lot of the one-hand open position (that is, not much body contact). I'm not sure if classes in blues dancing would be a good choice for a total newbie, so if you've never had a dance class in your life, check with the teacher first. There are a number of blues dancing videos on YouTube; check 'em out (when I wrote this book, there was even one of ballrooming titled "Friday Night Blues— Ballrooming Demo").

Slow dancing can be an easy dance to pull off because it's so forgiving. It's a loose form of dance; there's not much curriculum and there's not much competition, so there's not much to judge. Goof around a bit and nobody will care; it may even get praise. If you do it with a stranger, just start with a little separation (between your bodies) and try to have fun. You might be surprised what develops.

## Do a Dip

I'm not going to attempt to teach a *dip* in a book, but I want to psych you up to learn to dip. A dip is easy, it's eye-catching, you can use it in every dance—especially a slow dance—and it's great for expressing musicality. Did I mention that many women love to dip?

A dip may look hard, but for all the excitement it creates, I find there isn't much to do. For a simple dip, there aren't a lot of weight changes or twirling body parts, which makes it an easy move for me. The hardest part is phrasing and musicality, timing it to a good spot in the music, which will be easy once you can hear the sets of 8. While a dip is an obvious move to end a dance, you can usually slip dips in at other spots, whenever the melody winds down a bit. (**ADVANCED INFO ALERT** Dip during the last set of 8 of a major phrase.)

To keep it simple, which is what you need to do when your partner or you are a beginner, you don't have to do a full dip; you can do a one-quarter dip or a one-eighth dip and still create nice-looking lines with your body, while you avoid the risk of literally dropping your partner. I've never dropped a partner; but I've come close, either because I didn't know what I was doing or I had a no-fear follower who didn't know how to dip. (Ladies, there's a correct way to dip that allows you to hold your own weight.)

There is a variety of dips, so choose one that's easy to do. Practice doing a partial dip by just going into it 10 or 20 percent, enough to get a stretch in your body and create a nice line, but not enough that you could lose your balance and throw the whole experiment on the floor.

*Caution:* In addition to women who like to dip but don't know how, there are followers who don't like to dip and will resist—strongly, often by freezing their whole body rigid. This is understandable; probably some jerk in the past forced a dip and injured her. I do the first dip with an unknown partner slowly and gently, with the intention of not doing a full dip. I'm prepared to abort the move immediately if my partner turns stiff. I'm also prepared to accept her full body weight in case she wants to dip, doesn't know what she's doing and lunges into it.

# Chapter 13

# *Survival Dancing*

No mistakes in the tango, Donna darling, not like life. Simple, that's what makes the tango so great: if you make a mistake, get all tangled up, you tango on.

— *Al Pacino, in* Scent of a Woman

Not for a nanosec do I believe this dance stuff is easy, especially for the guy. I pose this question: Are you artistically and egotistically prepared to ask, embrace and dance with a dauntingly gorgeous stranger, in public, at the hippest joint in town, on an unfamiliar floor, to music you've never heard before, to a dance you don't know, surrounded by an ocean of gawking eyes? How about the boss's spouse, who has had too much to drink, at the company Christmas party? How about the groom's mother, who can't keep the beat, at a friend's wedding? How about your wedding dance—with a bride who likes to lead!

When you land in a deer-in-the-headlights situation, the order of battle is straightforward: survive the three minutes. My strategy is to keep it simple by doing a little footwork and not much more. Do that and you'll survive; do that well and you may win your partner's fancy.

Survival dancing can both rescue you from a nervous dance and sweep a lady off her feet. What follows applies to everything from slow dancing—basic slow dancing is just survival dancing to slow music—to surviving a dance you don't know, to doing an eye-catching, improvisational dance that might just be the envy of the floor. The ability to improvise is a lost art; and partners will line up if you do it well, especially when slow dancing. Survival dancing is a critical component of the Renaissance man's dance portfolio.

The easiest footwork to do is single and double rhythm, which, done in the closed position (Chapter 8, "Positions"), is the foundation of **survival dancing**. There are very few situations in which one of these three rhythm patterns can't save the moment:

**1.** all single rhythm

**2.** all double rhythm

**3.** *double—single—double—single*

Let's go through them one at a time.

If you've never danced before, if the thought of three minutes on a dance floor sounds worse than a night in prison, repeating single rhythm is a good choice for surviving a dance. (If you need a refresher, single rhythm was discussed on page 51 and marked on page 64.) While there's no formal dance that uses only single rhythm, it's often the default rhythm people attempt when they can't dance, because it involves the fewest steps yet still has some semblance of being a dance. I say "attempt" because most men who can't dance have poor timing and do not step on the beat. When it's done incorrectly, you just get an awkward rocking back and forth. When it's done with technique, you get a good-looking sway.

Looking at eight beats of music, this is a good verbal call to use: STEP TOUCH—STEP TOUCH—STEP TOUCH—STEP TOUCH. Starting with the weight on your right foot, slowly transfer your weight back and forth on every other beat. Weight changes occur on the downbeat (**counts 1**, **3**, **5** and **7**). Once you get the timing and basic footwork for single rhythm, you turn it into a sway through good movement technique (Chapter 9, "Movement and Timing") and by adding some body shaping. A sway with good timing and technique is what you want to do to improve the awkward high-school-prom-looking hug and sway from Chapter 12, "Slow Dancing."

*Freebie Video:* Check out my website if you want to see the footwork for single rhythm and the sway. This is YouTube–type stuff, so keep your expectations low.

While some may not acknowledge the sway to be a dance, I feel the step has legitimacy if done correctly—good technique and stepping on the beat. For a sensual slow dance, add some body contact. You can embellish a sway with a slow rotation in place. If you stay on the beat you'll survive; throw in a little conversation, maybe laugh a little, and you won't look half bad at a New Year's Eve party.

The next rhythm pattern for survival is repeating double rhythm. This is a step on every beat of music: STEP STEP—STEP STEP—STEP STEP—STEP STEP (for a refresher, see page 53). It's twice as many steps as single rhythm, so it's not a good choice for faster tempos. But it works well when the tempo is so slow that singles are awkward and feel like slow motion. You can use double rhythm both to shuffle in place and to travel around the floor in what is, essentially, a walking step. Repeating double rhythm can be easy because it feels the closest to walking; but I find it a bit monotonous and, if the tempo is a little too fast, tiring. I tend to use it for short periods, say four to sixteen beats of music, and then move on to different rhythm patterns.

There is one dance that uses all double rhythm: the merengue. And there's one situation when I repeat double rhythm through most of the dance: unidentifiable Latin music. I'm not much of a merengue dancer and I can't identify merengue music, but if I get stuck with unknown Latin music and nothing seems to work, the merengue rhythm pattern usually works for me. Note that I'm just using the merengue rhythm, *double—double,* but I'm not doing a merengue, the dance, by Latin dance standards. Essentially, I do a Latin march, just a STEP STEP—STEP STEP, which I keep repeating. I keep my steps small and tight, mostly dancing in place, and I usually do a slow rotation. I stylize it with a hint of Latin hips (emphasis on the word *hint*—I leave good hip motion to Latinos, and I leave exaggerated hip motion to competitors on *Dancing with the Stars*). If you want to do a lot of Latin dancing or if you're, say, going on a cruise with Latin music, I think it's good to know how to use the merengue rhythm. It's easy to do, it's easily adaptable to a lot of music, it's easy to mix in step

## More with Single Rhythm

Repeating single rhythm has been a lifesaver for me. I fall back on it, regardless of the dance, anytime I get lost. If I'm tired or confused, I often do this rhythm to regain my composure and to find the beat again. I'll go to it when my partner can't dance and nothing seems to work. I'll do it for eight beats or sixteen beats or whatever it takes to think through the problem, which might include cracking a joke to break the tension.

Doing all single rhythm is also one way to start a dance with a new partner, as it's a way to establish a dance connection. It's a way to make sure you're both in sync with each other and the music. You just sway back and forth in single rhythm for a handful of beats—however long it takes to connect to your partner and the music. Doing all single rhythm with some styling can look sharp.

I'll never be the best dancer on the floor—unless I'm at a wedding where nobody knows how to dance—but I strive to be a smooth and competent dancer, one who can handle any situation and one whom any follower would be happy to oblige. Using single rhythm has gotten me through many tight spots.

**ADVANCED INFO ALERT** I also use single rhythm to add musicality to my dance or kill time (complete a phrase of music). While any dance rhythm can be used that feels good, as a lazy dancer with no talent I find single rhythm to be an easy, mindless rhythm to insert in a pinch.

patterns from other dances and it works well on small, crowded dance floors.

Finally, survival dancing is at its best when you mix singles and doubles. One of the easiest and most versatile rhythm patterns, *double—single—double—single,* was first explored on page 65. This is the mother of all patterns. The Golden State Dance Teachers Association refers to it as the survival dance because it can be done to a vast range of tempos and musical genres. They also feel it's easier to do than all single rhythm as it fits the rhythmic pulse of the music better and, avoiding the monotony of all singles, it gives you something to groove on. *This is the rhythm pattern to try if you're faced with music or a dance you don't know.* A good verbal call is: STEP STEP—STEP TOUCH—STEP STEP—STEP TOUCH. This is a true eight-beat pattern, and it will feel best if you start this on the first beat of a set of 8.

Note that this is the same rhythm pattern used in salsa and rumba, and it's often used in foxtrot. Salsa applies it in a forward-and-back basic figure, rumba uses it in a box step and foxtrot travels around the floor with it. In the context of survival dancing, you can move any direction you want! If you want a simple step pattern to get you started, check out the side step on page 103.

Beyond *double—single—double—single*, you can mix single and double rhythm any way your feet feel like moving. Try *double—double—single—single*. Try *single—single—double—double*. Try *double—single—single* (that's a common six-count foxtrot pattern). Try anything. Don't worry about which direction to move, just shuffle around—taking tiny steps—and see what evolves. When you get a little bored, let go of her back with your right hand, lift your left arm up and I bet your partner will go under it to do an underarm turn. When you get bored with her underarm turn, lift up your left arm again and you can walk under it. It's that easy. Don't worry if you lose the beat during a turn, just re-sync with the beat when the turn is done. It's a wonderful world of improvisation once you can find the beat, can execute single and double rhythm and have a rudimentary grasp of leading. Over time, if you take lessons, you'll learn new moves that can be used to embellish your improvisational dancing. If you're a guy with some athletic coordination and visual smarts, you should be able to observe others and steal moves.

In this type of dancing, without an identifiable dance, without patterns to remember, I get a wonderful sense of freedom. I find that by removing the boundaries imposed by a conventional dance, which begs for a robotic memory of step patterns, I'm forced to dance creatively, out of the box, and I'm better able to match rhythms to what's going on in the music. Somebody stop me.

## EXERCISE 17: SHADOW DANCE

Standing in place, practice marking the rhythms discussed earlier to a variety of music: *single—single—single—single, double—double—double—double, double—single—double—single.* Also try making up a few new patterns, like *double—double—single—single, single—single—double—double* and *double—single—single,* and see how they fit the music. Especially try them to music with slower tempos until you get the hang of it. Then, as in Exercise 9 on page 66, randomly mix single and double rhythm, trying to catch the changing texture of the music. Let yourself flow, catching the mood changes instinctively. Try without trying. Eventually, shuffle around with tiny steps: forward and back, side to side, rotate left, rotate right, and anything else that works. Improvise. Keep the area tight and the steps small; an inch or two or three in this direction, an inch or two or three in that direction. Keep your speed and energy in sync with the feel of the music; become the music. Hold your arms up as if you were in the closed ballroom position. Now you're shadow dancing. See also the next Advanced Info Alert on blank rhythm and add it to this exercise.

**ADVANCED INFO ALERT** My style, both for survival dancing and when I'm trying to impress, is all about the economy of motion. Less is more; that's me. With that in mind, my favorite dance rhythm is the blank rhythm. A blank has no weight changes (for example, a HOLD HOLD), which is perfect for a lazy, reluctant dancer like me. What, no weight changes, aren't you just standing still looking like a dork? Maybe, but if it's stylized and used strategically, just two beats here or four beats there or six beats here and there, I think it's a lady charmer. For example, when the melody in the music slows down, I like to catch it with

## Shall We Fake a Waltz?

While it's hard to find an entire evening of waltz, it's common to have a waltz or two mixed into an evening of dance. Women love to waltz; so if you're out to impress, the waltz is a dance to consider learning. Because waltz music is different from all other dance music, the three survival patterns discussed earlier will not work. As a refresher, the basics of waltz are discussed on page 74.

Before I understood waltz music, I identified waltzes through elimination. If I was unable to count sets of 8, I would try to count sets of 6 by listening for an emphasis on the **count 1s** and **count 4s**. If that worked, if I could count sets of 6, it was a waltz. If that didn't work, if I couldn't count sets of 6 or sets of 8, it was probably not dance music or, at least, not good dance music for me.

You can muddle your way through a waltz by marking the rhythm, that is, by stepping in place. Focus on hearing the sets of 6 and nailing down the beat; twirling around the floor will get no respect if you're off the beat. If the tempo is slow enough, just step on every beat. As you mark the rhythm, try to capture the rise and fall, the *down up up* feeling, with small movements of your body. If the tempo is uncomfortably fast, mark the rhythm by stepping on just the downbeats, **count 1** and **count 4**, which tend to be emphasized in the music. The **1** and **4** also have the down feeling, which you can dance to by dropping down just a tad on those beats. A good verbal call is: STEP TOUCH HOLD—STEP TOUCH HOLD (no weight changes on the TOUCH and HOLD). Again, don't worry about twirling, but if you can handle it, try a slow rotation in place. If people are traveling around the floor and knocking into you, move toward the center of the floor.

Because of the distinctive *down up up* feeling to waltz, it's a genre of music that's relatively easy to hear without counting and analysis. Try to get a feel for a waltz; once you listen to eight or ten waltzes from different musical genres, it may ignite your brain and you'll get it. Bop over to iTunes and sample some of these: *What the World Needs Now* (Dionne Warwick), *I'll Be* (Edwin McCain), *Iris* (Goo Goo Dolls), *Kiss from a Rose* (Seal), *Breakaway* (Kelly Clarkson),

> *Are You Lonesome Tonight* (Elvis Presley*), Take It to the Limit* (The Eagles), *Three Times a Lady* (The Commodores), *Open Arms* (Journey) and a couple of classics, *Moon River* and *Tennessee Waltz*. Note that not all music structured in sets of 6 makes you want to waltz.

a dramatic pause in my dancing, which I do with a blank rhythm or two. And there's nothing like catching a resolution in the musical phrasing—a thematic closure or ending in the melody—with a dip, which requires a blank rhythm or two. My execution of this stuff is not perfect. I often start late, and I'm late to resume dancing. But even being half a beat behind feels better—to both myself and my partner—than ignoring the music. And, funny thing, the more I try to connect to the music the tighter I get. Advanced dancers know that the musical structure of a song will repeat throughout the song. If you pay attention in the beginning, you can improve your musicality and connection to the music as the song progresses. *Advanced Exercise:* Play around with blank rhythm by adding it to the mix in the shadow dancing exercise (Exercise 17).

I can't over-emphasize the versatility of mixing single and double rhythm when you get into a pinch. As a beginner, one of the conundrums of dance is that even if you know some dances, very often you can't identify the music. As you look at other couples for clues, usually a good trick, there may be no consensus. You'll have to do something and *double—single—double—single* is a good place to start. After a moment, if the music genre becomes clear and it's a dance you know, you can transition to it. If not, just stay connected to the sets of 8, shuffle around with singles and doubles and try to connect to the mood of the music and your partner.

# Chapter 14

# Surviving the Wedding Dance

If someone came up to me and said, "Real men don't dance," I'm gonna tell him real men try to do things that they think they cannot do, and that's the difference between another man and a real man.

— Emmitt Smith, three-time Superbowl champion,
NFL's all-time leading rusher, winner
of ABC's Dancing with the Stars

You're getting married and you'll have to dance. There will be a crowd and there will be cameras. A little planning and practice will make the video fun to watch for the rest of your life (as you know, people with cell phones will shoot video, whether you like it or not). Don't think of it as work, think of it as . . . oh, I don't know . . . foreplay.

Guys, buck up. Affirm the unwritten, male credo: *I can do anything*. Be James Bond. Learn an easy step or two, and it will get you through your wedding—and every other wedding, dinner dance, cruise, holiday celebration and covert spy operation you attend for the rest of your life.

If you have the time and the inclination, you can put together a decent dance and, if you have a hint of talent and like to perform, you can put on a show and wow the crowd. Wedding choreographers are gaining popularity; you can search them on the web.

But that's not our game. We're not about show; we're about survival. That means doing a survival dance (Chapter 13, "Survival Dancing")—if anyone asks, tell them it's a foxtrot—and focusing on the easiest step pattern known to man: the side step (page 103).

The side step makes a good foundation pattern—the pattern you do most of the time—for an easy-to-execute wedding dance. If you do this pattern as you smile and look into your partner's eyes, maybe exchange a few words and laugh a little, you'll get by. If you embellish the side step with a few extra moves, you'll look pretty good. Then, for the rest of your life, you'll always have a dance to pull out of your macho bag of tricks. People will look at you and think, *socializes well, not afraid to dance, he's cool, could be an alpha male.*

If you want to add stuff to the side step, here are things to try: a slow rotation; underarm turns (page 102); add another easy pattern like the box step (page 101); know how to do a sway (page 119), which you can fall back on anytime you get lost or bored or distracted (like talking—it's hard to talk and dance); add styling, even something as simple as pausing (use blank rhythm, pages 66 and 123) and gazing deeply into your partners eyes; throw in a dip (page 117) and I bet the crowd goes wild. But don't freak out. Just start with a basic side step with a slow rotation, plus a couple of underarm turns, and see what develops.

If you work with a teacher, there will be a temptation to add a lot of choreography, perhaps more than you can handle. You have to find the balance between doing too much and too little choreography and the balance between doing hard and simple choreography. Some amount of choreography is good; just knowing when to start the dance will help you—this sounds dumb—to start the dance. If you're rhythmically challenged, knowing when to start a dance isn't easy (see my rant on page 37). A little choreography will help you connect to the music and dance on time (on the beat). Dancing with no choreography might work for some, but it requires that you think on your feet; and, if you're rhythmically challenged, there's a greater chance you'll end up off time (not on the beat).

If you're not up to it, avoid stringing difficult moves one after another. Instead, work with your teacher on a bare bones choreography; ace that before getting too cute with the lifts, drops and triple-whammy-whatever kind of moves. What's simple choreography? Keep repeating an easy step pattern over and over, like the side step or the box step, then change to a new step pattern when the music changes (for example, when the music goes from a verse to the chorus). Keep repeating the new step pattern until the music changes again. Catching four or five changes in the music will look sharp; less will be more. Learn an easy dip and use it—not only to end the dance but in the middle, too, at a spot when the melody winds down or resolves. Spend time with your teacher on the basics, like improving your dance connection (page 94) and timing (dancing on the beat), which will improve the look of every move you do for the rest of your lives together. By matching the routine to your ability, you'll be more relaxed and you'll flow better—you'll be more in the moment, which will be reflected by the peaceful expression on your face.

To get started, choose your music carefully (see box "The Wedding Music"), then spend time alone with that song, counting sets of 8 (Chapter 2, "Counting Music: Finding the Sets of 8"). Practice shadow dancing, on your own, as described in Exercise 17 (Chapter 13, "Survival Dancing"), which will help your connection to the music and your ability to improvise, which will prove handy if you forget your routine. If you want to do a specific dance, the music will dictate what dance you do. Don't be set on a dance until you choose the music, and it's best to discuss it all with a teacher. For example, slow romantic songs may or may not be a waltz; some are in sets of 6, some are in sets of 8, but waltz can only be danced to music that's counted in sets of 6.

If you want to do choreography with a teacher, give yourself some months to get ready. Ideally, start group classes six months or so before the event. This will engage you in the process and give you time to gain comfort on the floor. Then take some private lessons a few months in advance so you can plan the dance, work on problem areas and make it all look good.

Some pointers, tips and reminders:

- Resist the temptation to bite off too much material. You'll look much better performing a few things done extremely well than you will doing many things poorly. Overall you may still look great, but there's no choreography that looks great if you're off the beat.

- Consider the size of the dance floor and make sure your choreography fits.

- Practice the routine in your wedding clothes and shoes. Try to practice once on the actual wedding floor to get a feel for how your shoes glide, or don't glide, across the floor.

- Go out dancing socially, so you can practice dancing spontaneously and dancing under the pressure of the spotlight.

- Videotape a practice session to see what needs work.

- Make sure your fiancée is learning to dance too. If she can't follow—if she's off the beat or doesn't give you a good dance frame or tries to lead—it's going to make it hard for you and hard for the partnership to look good.

- If the music is a digital file like a CD or an iPod, have a backup copy. Test it on the sound equipment prior to the wedding.

- Plan an entrance, which you'll want to coordinate with your deejay or band. For example, you may want to walk onto the floor arm in arm and then have the music start, or you may want to have the music start first and meet in the middle. Plan if you want someone to announce the beginning of the first dance.

- Tell your photographer in advance how you will

## The Wedding Music

There are many good choices for a wedding song; it's a personal preference. There are plenty of websites that give recommendations for the first dance as well as all the other music you'll need throughout the day: ceremony, cocktails, dinner, mother–son dance, father–daughter dance, cake cutting, garter toss, reception party, last dance, and so on. Search the web for "wedding dance music" and "first dance music."

Not every song that's recommended will be easy to dance to. So, even though this sounds like a no-brainer, choose music that's danceable. Choose something that you can get into and tap your foot to, something with a beat you can hear, and something with a comfortable tempo. Sometimes something too slow can be difficult, because you tend to rush the dance. Also, slow music will expose mistakes more readily. Choose a song that's enjoyable and meaningful, as it'll be easier to dance to.

The wedding dance is generally two to three minutes in length, so cut yourself a break and edit it down to two minutes. If it's a live band, don't forget to tell them to keep it to two minutes. Also, listen to the live band play the song before the wedding, so you know their tempo—it may be a little different from what you've practiced. If you want to impress, study the phrasing (page 36) of the music so you know where to start patterns and when to dip. Know your music well.

make an entrance and if there are highlights you want captured throughout the dance.

- If you forget your routine, go into a sway (STEP TOUCH—STEP TOUCH). If you're desperate to kill time on the floor, whisper something in her ear and laugh.

- Plan the length of the first dance and tell the band or deejay. Plan the ending and the transition to the next activity. Plan if you want other family members to join you on the dance floor, for example, if you want the father of the bride to cut in. Plan if you want this to happen during your song or the next song; plan the next song. Plan if and when you want the deejay to invite all your guests to join you on the dance floor.

- If you plan, not only will it go smoother and will you be assured that key moments are captured on film, you'll be more relaxed and confident going into the event.

- Mistakes are rarely noticed and everything, even a mistake, looks better if it's done with a smile.

Finally: Give a man a wedding routine and he dances for a day, teach a man some rhythm and he dances for a lifetime. I just made that up. My point is this: You can robotically choreograph a routine with a teacher and you'll do a decent job on your wedding day. I'm okay with that. But I also urge you to develop a foundation in music and rhythm. Learn to hear the beat in all music, not just your wedding song. Not only will your wife appreciate it every time you step on the floor, it's a gift to yourself, as it'll make listening to music more enjoyable.

# Chapter 15

# 16 Tips for Surviving a Dance

In city after city across the U.S., a new generation of tango dancers is packing the floor again. They swerve and kick, not to the traditional violins of, say, the great Francisco Canaro's orchestras, but to the dub beats of Massive Attack or wailing guitar lines of Jimi Hendrix. Formal wear is out; sneakers, low-rider jeans and halter tops are in.

— The Wall Street Journal, *August 29, 2005*

I have a theory: It's more embarrassing, and it takes more effort, to avoid dancing than it does to man up and lead a lady through a shuffle or sway for three minutes.

I came to this conclusion after years of stubbornly refusing to dance. I avoided the floor and often lurked in the corner, trying to hide that I'm-on-death-row look. I always had the suspicion that people were looking at me and thinking, *wow, that guy's got issues, he probably doesn't socialize well.* Guys, think about it: You may stand out more by refusing to dance.

Even if you can't dance, there are things you can do on the floor, not to dance, but to impress her with your character. For example, be confident. Whether you're bothered or not bothered by your lack of ability—it reveals character. For example, be gentle. Whether you're gentle or rough on the floor reveals character. For example, be supportive. Whether you criticize or compliment reveals character. For example, just show up. Many men won't even venture onto the floor; so getting out there, taking a risk, will score points. Conversely, a good dancer can easily deliver a bad experience by being egotistical, insensitive and rough.

Yeah, there's a learning curve in dance and you'll stumble around for a while. But looking back, the only stupid thing I did was sit out too many dances. It just made my path to being a guy who can do anything, including satisfying a woman on the dance floor, take that much longer.

So, what else can the klutz who can't dance do? There are no great answers, and some of this is a review, but dig your shoe leather into this:

**1.** *Wear the right clothes.* Clothes affect how you dance. Seriously. Clothes should feel right for dancing. I look for the following: freedom of movement; breathability (and comfort if you sweat); a good fit; the design of a garment so that it helps create nice body lines; and, as much as my style-challenged taste allows, fashionable garments. If you don't have any fashion sense, ask a woman to tell you what makes you look good.

I also consider clothes that fit the style of dance, such as sexy for the Latin dances, black for tango, retro for jitterbug, jeans for country and western. I tend to dress to fit the crowd. If you're self-conscious like me, being underdressed or overdressed can injure an evening; so while I rarely plead to conformity, I tend to wear what I think other guys will wear. Consider shoes with leather soles; they allow you to slide on a wood floor but still have some grip to help you stop. But, nowadays, great dancers dance in everything, including jeans, T-shirts and sneakers. So keep your options open. *Caution:* If you dance in shoes with rubber soles, be careful to not injure your knee when turning.

**2.** *Choose good music.* There's a lot of commotion in the beginner's mind, and it's easy to forget the music. Can I do my step patterns? Are there any cute partners here? Will she reject me? What dance should I do? How do I start the dance? But don't ignore the music, because the choice of music can make or break a dance. I need all the help I can get, so I'm always acutely aware of the music.

Not all music at a dance event will be easy to dance to; if you're only going to dance to a few songs, pick the better songs. If you're at a place with some dancing that's not a dedicated dance venue, be picky, as not all music is danceable. The jazz music of Count Basie, known as swing, is good dance music; but the jazz of Miles Davis, known as bebop, is not dance music at all. A jazz band may play a mix of swing and bop.

Most important, make sure you can hear the beat of the music. If you can't hear it or you're not sure, consider it a song to sit out. Also, choose a tempo that is slow enough to let you comfortably keep time. When I was a beginner, choosing a comfortable tempo was very important; while a great song won't guarantee a great dance, the wrong song, like something too fast, could ruin a dance for me. I also listen for an enjoyable melody, a simple and obvious structure that repeats throughout the song and good execution (a bad sound system can make the beat hard to hear). The music needs to be something I can get into, something that naturally makes me tap my foot. Choosing music you enjoy will loosen you up; it'll distract you from your nervousness, and it'll be easier to stay on the beat.

**3.** *Choose the right partner.* One of my worst experiences was with a partner, a much better dancer than I, who scolded me at the end of an awkward dance: "You need to be more sure of yourself." While she was right, the point of my little story is that sometimes you choose a bad partner. Sometimes you choose someone who is hard to dance with or she has a bad attitude or she just looks unhappy and it puts the kibosh on a fun time.

A good strategy is to study the dance floor and choose a partner who is about your level (although it's hard to be objective about your level if you're a beginner or have a big ego). If you're fearful of being rejected, look for someone who dances a lot of dances with a lot of different partners, including dancers of your ability. Someone you've danced successfully with in the past is usually a safe choice.

I also look at her proximity to the dance floor and body language. I don't have any scientific data to back this up, but I'll bet a hundred bucks that the nearer someone is to the dance floor, the more interested she is in dancing. And I'll bet a thousand smackers that someone standing right next to the dance floor, smiling and tapping her foot, will dance with anybody.

If you want to show off to the crowd, choose a partner who is better than you and who you've danced with before. If you want to impress your dance partner, choose someone who is of lesser ability than you; but remember, don't out-dance her. That will just piss her off (see tip number 7).

*Bonus Tip:* For guys, it's not a good strategy to wait to be asked to dance, especially if you're just a beginner. Even though women ask men to dance, the vast majority of the time, guys are still doing the asking. In general, the more you're seen on the floor, the greater the chance you'll be asked to dance, especially if you can dance well. If you're a reluctant dancer, force yourself to break the ice early in the evening, as it'll set the pace, both in your mind and with the crowd.

**4.** *Practice etiquette.* Knowing etiquette will minimize nervousness and help confidence. Some etiquette is specific to dance, such as moving counterclockwise around the floor for the traveling dances. And some etiquette is basic social interaction that follows the Golden Rule (do unto others as you would have them do unto . . . blah blah), plus some common sense and, occasionally, a dash of old-fashioned chivalry.

Chivalry? I don't like to get sappy, but I think it's handy to know how to fake it, because you become a more desirable partner. To keep it fun (for me), I punctuate that traditional behavior with an almost imperceptible grin. I also use it to my advantage. For example, when I ask a lady to dance, I do what's not uncommon, which is to extend my hand as if I were some knight in armor. Corny, sure, but it works well—it shows confidence—and it's all part of the show. I then lead the lady onto the floor, still holding her hand. In addition to the manly gesture of leading her by the hand through the crowd, by the time we get to our spot, I've already established a physical connection and I usually know what kind of dancer she'll be.

**5.** *Step first with your left foot.* For review, let's see how much I can cram into one paragraph: Start on a **count 1** or a **count 5** of the music (that will be hard to do until you hear the sets of 8; see Chapter 2, "Counting Music: Finding the Sets of 8"). Move from your solar plexus first; said another way, let foot follow frame. With the weight on your right foot, take the first step of a dance with your left foot (ladies with the right). Your right hand should cup the base of her left shoulder blade, and it should stay there, like you had a pillow wedged between your hand and chest. Hold her gently and avoid arm leads, which is leading by using your arms to push and pull her around. An easy step pattern to try is the eight-beat side step (page 103), which is just a side-to-side shuffle: SIDE TOGETHER—SIDE TOUCH—SIDE TOGETHER—SIDE TOUCH. In the face of disaster, attempt a basic sway (page 119): STEP TOUCH—STEP TOUCH—STEP TOUCH—STEP TOUCH (no weight changes on the TOUCH).

**6.** *Mimic other dancers.* In my early years of dancing, I relied heavily on mimicking other dancers. I cheated by finding a competent-looking couple and imitating what they were doing. Not only could I identify what dance to do, I copied exact footwork to get me on the beat and to get the correct rhythm going in my feet. When I sat out a dance, I studied others to refresh my memory on step patterns and styling and, after I had some degree of comfort with my dancing, to steal patterns and styling moves. Mimicry is a top survival skill; learn it well.

*Bonus Tip:* When you first arrive at a dance venue, observe the dance floor and see what others are doing; then match your ability to the situation.

**7.** *Dance at your partner's level.* Don't out-dance your partner—it's not fun for her, it makes the partnership look bad and she will not be anxious to dance with you again. If you're gentle and dance to make the partnership look good, she'll come back for more. If she can't dance, keep it simple; she will not be impressed that you know how to Lindy Hop if you drag her through it. Most guys have egos and want to show off. They want to impress her with their 32-volume Britannica of moves. But it's not cool to force-feed her patterns. Worse, if she can't follow a lead, most guys will strengthen the lead—they will use more force. That's not good dancing. A skilled and desirable leader will lighten the lead. He will dance with her, not around her. He will go with her flow. He's gentle, like the horse whisperer.

Make your partner feel good. It's hard to look good as a couple when your partner has a dirty look on her face. The late Frankie Manning, the grandfather of swing dancing, gives this advice: "You're going to be in love with this lady for three minutes." It doesn't matter that she models for Halloween masks, be charming: smile, make good eye contact, compliment her, don't push and drag her around the floor, don't have high expectations—have fun. This is particularly important when dancing with a woman who can't dance, as she's most vulnerable. But all partners need to be treated with consideration; don't be so into yourself that you ignore your partner and treat her like a sack of potatoes. Roughness is a prelude to injuries, so be gentle and concerned about her physical well-being. Bottom line: if your partner's not having a good time—look at her face for fear, confusion or disgust—stop what you're doing and try something else.

## Take Care of Your Partner

Really. It's not a competition; it's a partnership. Pssst . . . hey you, the one followers talk about behind your back . . . yeah, you. Here are more ways to help you work together:

- A good leader often shows off his follower. To use an old teaching metaphor, she's the picture, you're the frame. It's also referred to as letting your partner shine.

- Don't criticize or try to correct. If you tell your partner she's doing something wrong, even if you're right, you'll only antagonize her. This is especially true with strangers. I know, guys love to be problem-solvers because it makes us feel like big-shot, macho know-it-alls. But, as in life, you can only fix yourself. Every guy thinks a less-skilled partner wants a lesson, on the spot. Not only is that misguided, teaching on the floor is bad etiquette. Worse, there's a good chance she won't understand your advice but will still have her feelings hurt. If she asks for help, at least move off the dance floor (at the very least, move to an uncrowded edge of the floor).

- Be careful trying out a new move—I've ambushed partners with new patterns, and it can get ugly fast. Yes, even your humble guide and author has tweaked out a partner's shoulder. I find it best to practice my lead on a new pattern in private, or at least with a partner I know and to music with a slower tempo.

**8.** *Take small steps.* I mean teeny-tiny steps. Taking small steps is always less work and less stress. More important, it looks better. See the box on page 89.

**9.** *Keep good posture and dance frame.* Beginners are often easily identified by their poor posture and dance frame. For heaven's sake, stand up straight and strut a little. The muscles in your upper body should have tone: not too rigid and not too limp.

**10.** *Choose the right spot to dance.* There are two situations to consider when staking out some turf—hiding from onlookers to avoid embarrassment and avoiding traffic:

- Feeling embarrassed? Self-conscious? Don't be. In my early years, when I didn't want to be seen by anyone on the sidelines, I always waited for a crowded dance floor and, once on the floor, moved to the center of the pack or the back of the floor, where I couldn't be seen. A crowd was my friend. How we change: today, I love to seed an empty dance floor.

- *In a traffic jam?* If the floor is very crowded and there's a problem with people bumping into you, employ some floorcraft, the art of maneuvering through traffic. By moving around there's a good chance you'll find a spot that has fewer people. Always be prepared for your follower to give you a little tug or check on the back of your right shoulder, which means you were moving into a collision that you couldn't see. If people are traveling around the perimeter of the floor and you're getting in the way, move toward the center where people dance slower, or move to the center where people dance in one spot. If you have a collision, the proper etiquette is to apologize, even if it's not your fault.

**11.** *Look at your partner; don't look at your feet.* It's common for beginners to look at their feet, which looks bad and can become a bad habit. It's always best to keep your head up. Even better is to make eye contact and to do it often—short of giving her that stalker stare. Constantly looking at other dancers on the floor is a quick way to annoy your partner.

**12.** *Smile and look confident.* It doesn't have to be a big toothy grin, just a composed facial expression that says you're sure of yourself and are having a good time—something to hide the nervousness and fear.

## Where's My Step List?

In my early years, when I went to a dance, I always carried a step list—a list of moves I wanted to remember. Over time, I realized that I hardly ever looked at the list. I don't know why I ignored it; maybe it was too much work or I forgot about it or I felt embarrassed. But I wrote a list, kept it in my pocket and felt naked if I didn't have it. It gave me great comfort. Embrace the little, idiosyncratic rituals you do, as they can help calm the mind and relax you.

Can you be both confident and someone who can't dance and still make it all look good? Yes. I always remember the jealousy I had watching an inept and clueless couple who had zero ability and danced with total abandon. They were into themselves, had big smiles on their faces and could care less that they were off the beat and didn't know diddly about dance. Yet they caught my admiration, as well as the admiration of the group I was with, because they were having fun and were secure with what they were doing. I think the only time you look embarrassingly bad is when you're uptight and bothered by your inability to dance. So, if you flat out can't dance, the solution is not so much faking the dance, which requires some skill; the secret is faking your confidence.

**13.** *Ignore mistakes; laugh in the face of disaster.* A mistake generally feels much bigger than it looks, so if you recover without fanfare—don't stop and restart, dance right through it—it could easily go unnoticed (also see page 17). It's common to feel spotlighted when you dance; but it's unlikely many people, if any, are watching. Keep a light attitude; be able to laugh at yourself so when you make a mistake your reaction is to flash a genuine smile. If I stumble I try to laugh a little, as if we had just exchanged a funny joke and it was my uncontrollable laughter that made us trip. It looks better than getting all huffy and bent out of shape when you goof.

**14.** *Talk while you dance.* Yeah, I know, it's really not good form to talk and dance. And you can expect other dancers, including myself, to be annoyed if you stop dancing in the middle of the floor and just talk. Never do that. But a little chitchat while you dance is common, fun and suave—after all, if you can tell jokes while twirling through patterns, maybe you can do anything. In the context of survival, exchanging a few words can help to cover your inability to dance; that is, entertain her with your wit, not your choreography. If you can't dance, exchanging some pleasant words as you do an awkward sway will look better than exchanging dirty looks as you do an awkward sway. If you can dance and want to talk, you may have to dumb down to simpler moves because talking will distract your dancing.

Keep the talk light and constructive. Comment on the music. Crack a joke. Flirt a little. Let her know you enjoy dancing with her. It's always appropriate to compliment her dancing: "You move nicely," or, if she can't dance, try something like "You have the potential to become an excellent dancer." Complimenting her may even have a placebo effect and enable her to dance better.

**15.** *Don't burden yourself.* When you go out for an evening of dance, don't overwhelm yourself with things you want to remember to practice, as you'll probably forget them all anyway. I find it best to work on only one thing in an evening.

**16.** *Relax.* In my early years I could make Vice President Al Gore look like the rubberband-man. Granted, it's hard to relax when you're just a beginner. Nonetheless, tension will make your dancing stiff; relaxation will make your dancing look effortless. Would you rather be a stiff guy who can't dance or a relaxed guy who can't dance?

# *Reality Check*

O kay, let's regroup. Time for a reality check. Let's look at what you're really going to encounter on a dance floor.

Most people can't dance. This includes most women. This includes most people who say they know how; maybe six months of lessons a few years back looms large in their ego, but it doesn't mean beans today. I could even make an argument that most people currently taking dance classes can't dance (by definition, a beginner in an activity does not do it well, and it could take the average person a couple of years of dance classes to reach the intermediate level).

On an unsophisticated dance floor, like a wedding, there are decent odds your partner will be rhythmically challenged. Her timing may be so bad that it screws up your lead. You may be barely able to control her if she hears the beat of a different drum (insists on a beat or rhythm in the music that does not exist) or gives you no dance frame (spaghetti arms) or has been boozing it up. She's probably never learned to tango. I doubt she knows how to cha-cha. I'd be shocked if she could Lindy Hop or West Coast swing. So even if you know how to cha-cha, you may be unable to pull off the basic step pattern. If she can do the basic, that may be all you get out of her and your textbook of moves will go unused.

At a wedding or a New Year's Eve party, awkwardness is average. If you stumble a little through a dance, that's normal. But if you're gentle and don't try to rip her arm off, she'll probably think you're an okay dancer. If you can stay on the beat and can do one basic pattern, that's probably going to impress her. In general, just a modicum of competency will serve you well. And dance is relative; if you're just a little better than the last guy—remember, most guys can't dance—she'll think you're a good dancer. So, in casual dance situations, where nobody knows how to dance, you generally don't need a lot of ability. Just don't rip on her arm; that really ticks them off.

I know, juggling all the information in this book will be hard to do. And if you're like me in my early years, you'll forget everything you've learned the moment you step on the floor. If the thought of dancing in public, in the spotlight, unnerves you, find some comfort in the notion that onlookers only watch the best dancers. Hear that? Nobody's watching if your dancing sucks.

# Quick Definitions

*Note:* Words are arranged in roughly the order that they appear in the book.

## MUSIC

**beat** the underlying beat; the pulse of the music, which usually comes from the drums

**tempo** the speed of the music, usually stated in beats per minute (BPM)

**on time** a weight change occurring precisely on the beat is on time; if you're early or late, it's off time

**set of 8** eight beats of music, which, thematically, sound like a "sentence" of music; virtually all dance music is structured in sets of 8 (waltz, the exception, is structured in sets of 6); counting sets of 8 is the only way to confirm you found the beat; two four-beat measures are naturally paired to create a set of 8; a set of 8 is also called a *mini-phrase*

**counting music** counting the beats in the sets of 8 (sets of 6 for waltz)

**count 1** the first beat of a set of 8; also called "the **1**" for short; the second beat is **count 2**, the third beat is **count 3**, and so on

**downbeat** and **upbeat** when dealing with sets of 8, beats are naturally paired, a downbeat followed by an upbeat (waltz is structured in threes, downbeat upbeat upbeat); the downbeats are **counts 1**, **3**, **5** and **7** and the upbeats are **counts 2**, **4**, **6** and **8**

# RHYTHM

**verbal call** the language used to call a step pattern as you dance, which varies from teacher to teacher; the same step pattern can have different verbal calls, which can get confusing; in this book, STEP and TOUCH are the two verbal calls used most often (see other definitions in this section)

**step** a weight change; note that a weight change can be done in place; step is a common word, and the meaning needs to be taken in context; also see next entry, STEP

**STEP** a verbal call that indicates a weight change; a STEP is the instant the weight changes and not the process of taking a step

**TOUCH** a verbal call that indicates a beat of music with no weight change; instead of transferring your weight to the unweighted foot, simply touch the unweighted foot to the floor—an action with no weight change—which gives you something to do on the beat of music to help you stay connected to the beat

**HOLD** another verbal call that indicates a beat of music with no weight change (that is, it's similar to a TOUCH)

**QUICK** and **SLOW** extremely common verbal calls but not used in this book because of limitations (see box on page 53); when used correctly, a QUICK QUICK is two beats of music and is usually interchangeable with a STEP STEP (a double rhythm); a SLOW is also two beats of music and is usually interchangeable with a STEP TOUCH or a STEP HOLD (a single rhythm)

**dance rhythm** the number of weight changes in two beats of music (except waltz, see pages 74 and 121), for example, single rhythm, double rhythm

**single rhythm** one weight change in two beats of music; common verbal calls are STEP TOUCH and STEP HOLD; looking at just the first two beats of music, the pattern count would be: **1 hold–2**

**double rhythm** two weight changes in two beats of music; a common verbal call is STEP STEP; looking at just the first two beats of music, the pattern count would be: **1 2**

**triple rhythm** three weight changes in two beats of music; common verbal calls are STEP-THREE-TIMES and TRIPLE-STEP; looking at just the first two beats of music, the pattern count would be: **1&2**

**blank rhythm** no weight changes in two beats of music (HOLD HOLD); see more on pages 66 and 123; looking at just the first two beats of music, the pattern count would be: **hold-1 hold-2**

**rhythm pattern** a combination of two or more dance rhythms; for example, salsa and rumba, which share the same rhythm pattern, is *double—single—double—single*

**step pattern** a combination of the rhythm pattern and the direction

**direction** direction of movement, which includes foot positions (feet together, feet shoulder width apart, and so on)

**counting step patterns** identifying the sequence of weight changes in a step pattern by counting only the beats that have weight changes; counting a step pattern creates the *pattern count*

**pattern count** counting a step pattern, which identifies the sequence of weight changes, creates the pattern count; also referred to as the *count* for short; for example, the count for East Coast swing and West Coast swing is, **1 2—3&4—5&6**

**& count** a point between two beats of music; every beat of music has an **& count**, for example, **&1**, **&2**, **&3**; the **& count** is vocalized only if there's a weight change or action on that particular **& count**; for example, starting on **count 1**, the pattern count for dancing a triple rhythm, which is three weight changes, would be, **1&2**

**mark** doing weight changes in place; marking rhythm patterns is the best way to learn them

## DANCE

**dance frame** your stature, how you hold your arms in relation to your body, including the tone necessary to create a dance *connection* (page 94); think of tone as an energy level in your arms that's enough to keep them extended without falling down

**closed position** the familiar-looking embrace that's used in the basic step pattern of most social dances; this is the dance position used for survival dancing

**lead** and **follow** the primary way dancing couples communicate; a lead is an indication of direction; following is a reaction to a lead; traditionally men lead and women follow

**survival dancing** doing single and double rhythm in the closed position; the three rhythm patterns that will get you through most situations are: all single rhythm, all double rhythm, *double—single—double—single*; a side step (page 103) is an easy and versatile step pattern for survival; fall back on a sway (page 119) if nothing else seems to work

J ames Joseph used to hate to dance. In seventh grade, he was the only guy who refused to take social dancing. He was rhythmically challenged and counted his dance experience by sweaty palms and blushes—not by trophies won at dance competitions. He took his first beginners' class in 1984, and he may hold the record for the most beginners' classes ever taken. He's still taking them. Since 1996 he has trained under Skippy Blair, who is considered by many the teacher of teachers. His current aspiration in life is to become a geriatric ballroom dance gigolo on cruise ships—but he's not old enough so he kills time by writing. His prior books, all classics (in his mind, anyway), include *The Kreplachness Monster, Read Your Way to the Top* and *Working Wonders: 60 Quick Break Techniques to Beat Burnout, Boost Productivity and Revive Your Work Day.*

LaVergne, TN USA
13 January 2010
169817LV00004B/44/P